STIMULATING
STUDENT
SEARCH

STIMULATING STUDENT SEARCH

Library Media/Classroom Teacher Techniques

Hilda L. Jay

LIBRARY PROFESSIONAL PUBLICATIONS
1983

© 1983 Hilda L. Jay   All rights reserved
First published in 1983 as a
Library Professional Publication (LPP)
an imprint of The Shoe String Press, Inc.
Hamden, Connecticut 06514

Printed in the United States of America

Library of Congress Cataloging in Publication Data

Jay, Hilda L., 1921–
Stimulating student search.

Bibliography: p.
Includes index.
1. Library orientation—Study and teaching.
2. Libraries and students. 3. Instructional materials
centers. I. Title.
Z711.2.J33 . 1983   025.5′6   82-22916
ISBN 0-208-01936-7
ISBN 0-208-01926-X (pbk.)

Contents

Introduction   7

1. The Teaching Team's Responsibility
   to the Student   9

2. Insuring Materials Supply and Workflow   13

3. Choosing a Topic   20

4. Preparing for the Search   29

5. Reviewing Basic Skills   35

6. Organizing the Search Project   47

7. Search Projects and Activities   66

Index   175

Introduction

Twenty years spent in a school trying to assist students and classroom teachers and discussing mutual concerns as well as teaching and talking with other library media specialists have convinced me that the problems basic to the teaching of search skills to students have not been solved by very many people. It is the unusual classroom or subject teacher who has had the chance during preparation to teach to become confident in the use of the school library media center as an instructional resource. Staff development inservice sessions may be offered, but frequently they do not erase teacher reluctance to use library materials on a regular, intrinsic basis. Many teachers seem not to grasp that the development in students of the organizational skills necessary to make learning gratifying makes equally for improved teaching experiences for themselves. They remain hesitant to try, and students are still leaving high schools without being able to plan and execute a successful information search.

The term "search paper" is used throughout this book because it describes what the students really do. They search references in order to locate information which will help them to examine, analyze, reorganize, and synthesize as they create their papers and reports. True research, such as that done by advanced biology students carrying out self-devised experiments, does not enter into the construction of a search paper. On the other hand, neither should this paper be permitted to deteriorate into a mere collection of bits and pieces of information selected from various sources. There should be a significant element of thought and personal evaluation included so that students will have made a real contribution to the finished product themselves—if only to the implications and conclusions. To make thoughtful statements and to be able to support them on a solid information base is an essential skill to be acquired by any student anywhere.

The basic premise of this book is that doing search papers can

7

be enjoyable for both the student and the teacher. When the structure of the project is based upon the use of reference materials by types, the learning will apply across disciplines because these same types of references will be available in every discipline. Moreover, this process can be used successfully starting with fourth grade and going right on through graduate school. The process remains the same; the content is adjusted to the resources available and to the level and abilities of the students.

If a large number of references is available in a well-stocked library media center, the students will be introduced to a larger number of specific references, though probably not to a larger number of types of references. Indeed, even the school that has limited numbers of resources will be able to provide at least one example of each of the standard types of references, and this small number will be sufficient to introduce the processes described hereafter.

This book is intended primarily as a tool for the library media specialist or the classroom teacher who wants to make more effective use of the library media center as a teaching tool. It may also serve as a textbook for students studying in schools of library and information science or education. Students themselves who want to know more about the structure of search papers may also find it useful.

1. The Teaching Team's Responsibility to the Student

Acquiring search skills is a basic requirement for learning of any kind. Whether one's informational need is oriented to a hobby, running a business, improving or redecorating a residence, tax or legal problems, local political concerns, gardening, sewing or any other how-to purpose, the library media center will provide a variety of answers. If the need is academic, as in the case of higher education, good search skills utilized in a good library, are essential. Too often, however, this vital source and process for getting information are not used unless one has formed the habit of library use early in life. Competence in using reference tools leads to their use, not only during the years of formal education but throughout life. As information continues to proliferate and people must learn to live with rapid change, they should expect to revise and reorganize their marketable skills several times within a lifetime. The ability to keep currently and accurately informed is essential.

The schools must take a major responsibility for developing search skills in students. To be taught effectively, instruction and followup practice in searching for information and using it must become an all-hands endeavor. Teachers need to devise lesson plans which incorporate numerous learning activities that require search as an integral part; department heads have the responsibility to see to it that all teachers in their departments do in fact provide this opportunity; school principals must expect this type of activity and make its presence or absence a part of faculty evaluations; curriculum directors contribute by making certain that all curricular guides are written to include use and practice of basic search techniques; superintendents prove their commitment by emphasizing acquisition of search skills in goal statements for the system and in budgetary allotments for materials and staff, both professional and nonprofessional. All staff members need to become involved with the implementation of the program.

Efforts should be made to secure a curriculum approved by the board of education and integrated into each department's activity which requires the use of media and attendant skills. When a curriculum is being revised, the library media teachers as well as the classroom teachers should be involved. When no invitation is extended to the library media teachers to participate in curricular design, they may submit written samples of other school systems' integrated curricula along with examples that could be used in their own schools.

Because some grammar textbooks include a unit on use of the library, in the past the implication has been that it was the sole responsibility of an English department to carry the total burden of search instruction. This one unit is, of course, quite insufficient for the student and having it attached to only English coursework obscures the fact that the learning and use of these skills must permeate the entire curriculum and be a responsibility accepted by all classroom teachers regardless of subject taught. Certainly, the English department has a responsibility for making sure that students appreciate and can use the specialized references related to author biography, literary history, criticism, and allusion, but it is unreasonable to expect English teachers to instruct students in the use of materials more directly adaptable to use by other departments and disciplines. English teachers should not be made responsible for introducing specialized references in statistics, mathematics, science, social studies, art, music, history, and the like except as they might relate to the preparation of a specific paper for English class. It may require the firm determination and ongoing interest—even insistence—of administrators to insure that the basic specialized references for each discipline are introduced and used in the assignments made by the classroom teachers of each department.

Students fare best when the library media teachers and the classroom teachers work together in planning units, instructing the students, and helping them during workshop time spent in the library media center. Today's library media teachers recognize that their work with classroom teachers and with students in the classrooms is a major aspect of their jobs. This part of their work is no less important than the one-to-one work with students in the library or the technical processing and housekeeping that makes a collection functional. Library media teachers usually have a great willingness to meet with classroom groups to provide instruction in the use of materials. The class group may come to the library or the library media teacher may take a book truck filled with sources and go to the classroom. Either way, time spent in introducing a classroom group to basic search strategies allows the library media teacher to give more undivided attention to the individual student's unique needs in the center. If there has been good group instruction beforehand, a group can usually get started at once and make considerable progress in a search before requiring individual assistance. However, unless classroom teachers are receptive to having the library media teachers come into the classroom and plan lessons that require the use of these practical skills, there will be a less comprehensive learning experience offered and students will be shortchanged. The classroom teacher's attitude is a major factor either in instilling acute dislike for activity associated with the library media center or in creating an eager sense of challenge and accomplishment associated with searching for and using materials.

The floundering and frustration that arise from being merely taken to the library media center and told to "find something" can be devastating to a student. In contrast, a carefully structured series of lessons can be designed to give direction every step of the way. One segment is built upon another until each has meaning in the entire process. This approach will give the student the support needed to develop ultimately the confidence of a capable user of both print and nonprint media.

It is important for classroom teachers and library media teachers to realize that together they make up the most important part of the team which provides learning opportunities and skills for students. There are ways of planning search and writing assignments so that the teacher is not crushed under the load of papers to be graded and so that the ongoing program is not robbed of large amounts of time. The keys to this are integration and small segment assignments.

When each segment is a piece of a carefully planned whole, the completion of each segment is one step along the continuum. If the plan for the fourth quarter of the year is to write a paper which will include biographical, critical and historical elements of a topic, it is logical to have given instruction in the use of each type of reference material and to have called for an application of each along the way. Asking for biographical information about certain writers as they are being read would make an easy introduction. Later, finding evaluative statements about given works could lead to classroom enrichment. So could awareness of the period in which a writer, such as Dickens, wrote. Similarly, use of primary resources, periodical articles, and newspaper accounts could be the requirements for some other short papers. Brief excursions into topics associated with current classroom activity could introduce each of these types of references and their attendant indexing prior to their being used in combination for a lengthy paper.

Full integration with ongoing class content eliminates the feeling that everything stops while the "library lesson" takes place. Instead, those lessons become functional experiences. The resulting papers may be short ones and are graded as the marking period progresses, rather than being lumped together in one final "date due" deluge.

Students cannot learn these skills without practicing them. This practice must come as part of student work on regular assignments and not be "stuck on" to them in some meaningless way. Students should never be given the impression they are doing "a library assignment." Rather they should be learning that to do their work in any subject area they need certain skills and the ability to use the materials that are housed in a library media center. The approach should be: here is the source of information; locating information and using it is a challenge; achievement can be both satisfying and pleasurable. The feeling of drudgery can be omitted; independent learning and self-propelled forward movement can be rewarding— in school and throughout life.

2. Insuring Materials
Supply and Workflow

One of the principal causes of reluctance on the part of the classroom teacher to assign written projects is fear of the huge amount of time required to schedule and to grade a significant paper. Planning and timing can effectively reduce the strain. Some of this requires departmental cooperation, but much of it is controllable by the classroom teacher.

Students run into trouble when there is not enough material available. On questionnaires about search assignments, lack of sufficient materials rates high as a cause of disinterest and frustration among students. Classroom teachers have the responsibility to make sure that this does not happen to their students; close teamwork with the library media teachers will do wonders to remove the problem.

Classroom teachers can address the situation by, first, making sure that there is enough material available to the students to permit them a satisfactory experience, and second, staggering the load through careful timing and designing. Specific suggestions for accomplishing these tasks follow.

Textbook Bibliography

It does not help the student when the text suggests an activity and gives a bibliography to support that activity on which references are unavailable. Make sure that the school's collection can provide these items, or create an alternative list for students that will provide similar coverage with books that are available. This needs to be done *before* the assignment is made.

Syllabus

Caution is needed when the teacher provides a syllabus for the school term. Some students will look ahead and check out the best materials well in advance of their need for them. Classroom teachers who use a syllabus system may need to place all listed materials on reserve at the beginning of the term *before* the syllabus is distributed.

Otherwise, when the time comes to use the materials, there may be none to place on reserve.

Number of Items

When the teacher makes an original assignment, it is important to check with the library media teachers to see if the assignment can be supported properly. It makes a great difference whether one classroom group of thirty students or three or four sections of students will be trying to use the same materials at the same time. Also, be aware that although there may be a variety of topics given to the students, there will be an acute problem if the majority of the topics are treated in only one (or even several) books. The library media teachers should either be aware of additional items that can serve the same need or alert the classroom teacher that the center's resources are too meager to supply so many students at once. Quite possibly some other teacher, even in another department, may be in the midst of a project which requires the same materials. If this is the case, clearly a modification of plans is called for.

Coping with Short Supplies

BROADER LIST OF TOPICS. Add items to the topic list drawn from a larger than usual range of related areas. If the subject is a person or an event, bring in the social background, the arts, or parallel happenings in other countries. For example, when Shakespeare is being studied, think of more than his life and plays as topics. Other possibilities include contemporary sports, the law, the court, amusements, superstitions, handwriting, travel, the pubs, housing, the status of women or children, costume, or education. Events that took place in Shakespeare's lifetime (1564–1616) can be examined to frame his life, put his perceptions in context, and provide more perspective: the Peace of Troyes in the year of his birth, the conflict between Queen Elizabeth and Mary Tudor, the Spanish Armada, the Irish question (even then), the chartering of the East India Company, Guy Fawkes and the Gunpowder Plot, the activity of Boris Godunov in Russia, French exploration of Canada, Portuguese activity in Brazil and the founding of Rio de Janeiro, Raleigh's interest in Virginia, the London and Plymouth Companies of England, and the United East Indian Company of the Dutch.

BOOK TRUCK IN THE CLASSROOM. Take the limited number of materials to the classroom and assign groups of students to work on a subtopic together right there in the classroom. Perhaps four or five such subtopics will be enough, and a collection which provides a single reference per student is adequate when these can be exchanged and shared satisfactorily.

STAGGERED ASSIGNMENTS WITHIN EACH CLASS. Have one part of a classroom group do a segment of search and another part of the group do a later search to balance out experiences *within the same marking period.* Fewer students will need to use the same items simultaneously, but all students will get practice in the use of the materials. An example of this type of planning is found in the sophomore English search project on pages 116–117.

STAGGERED ASSIGNMENTS AMONG CLASSES. Have only one classroom section at a time do a search paper during each marking period. Materials go further and there are fewer papers to correct at any one time. The classroom sections need not work on the same subject content to gain comparable search skills.

EARLY SCHEDULING. Avoid waiting until the last quarter of the school year when all the other procrastinators make similar assignments. The students are not motivated to do their best work under these conditions.

SHORTER, DEVELOPMENTAL PAPERS. A classroom teacher should be able to assess how much preparatory work needs to be done with a group of students before assigning a long paper. Student skills need to be developed, and certain content should be covered before the search paper is really as beneficial to the students as it should be. Smaller beginning assignments can be planned so that they lead into and provide experience useful for the final paper. Examples of this type of assignment will be found in the final chapter of this book.

INTRADEPARTMENTAL PLANNING. To lessen the demand on any one type of reference, plan within the department so that several classroom teachers are not doing the same thing at the same time. Post a schedule in the departmental office or in the library media center and stagger the use of the materials. English departments can work within format, even within the same time period, and still alleviate overcrowding by using different genres for the search project. Plays, poems, novels, essays, biographies, and letters all produce helpful diversity and lead students to a variety of references. If one classroom teacher works with novels and another with dramas while a third chooses poetry, the library media collec-

15

tion will serve many more students simultaneously and effectively. Social studies departments can develop diversity with the use of different time periods or geographic areas and by incorporating more than the traditional history books as needed references. Pulling from art, music, travel, costume, and all the other aspects of social history will broaden the interest among searchers as well as provide a practical broad base of usable materials. The assignments made for Medieval and Renaissance history on pages 148 through 157 are excellent examples of this technique.

Easing the Teacher's Correction Load

Now let us consider ways of making the teacher's life easier and more interesting when the papers must be evaluated. In order to have fewer papers to read at any one time, the following possibilities should be considered:

DUE DATES SPREAD THROUGHOUT THE TERM OR YEAR. When a major search paper assignment is made early, to run throughout the term, it is helpful to designate dates due for presentations throughout the entire term. These dates should be posted with the topic, and the dates should correspond with the class plan so that students will be reporting at a time when the content of their papers provides supplementary information for classroom discussion. The students should know the due dates when they accept the topic. Often students are preparing papers or projects in their other classes and appreciate the opportunity to spread their academic load just a little. From the teacher's point of view, the grading load is spread out over the entire term. The plan shown on page 140 exemplifies this concept.

SHORTER PAPERS. Several shorter papers tend to teach more than one long paper. This is not to say that lengthy term or search papers do not have a valuable place in the student's experience; they do. However, there is need for a variety of smaller, shorter exercises than can be evaluated by the teacher both to provide guidance and gradual growth and to build up the student toward undertaking a long paper. If the student has but one paper assigned for the year and something goes wrong with it, much of the learning experience is lost in panic and frustration. The school year is over, as likely as not, and there is no time to try again.

When classroom teachers make unstructured search paper assignments in September with due dates in June, on a topic of the students' choice that is not necessarily related to the subject content of the course, the student is usually headed for trouble. There may even be the temptation to use an old paper and update the bibliography a bit. There is an almost irresistible temptation to procrastinate, and the end result is often a rushed, thrown together, substandard scribbling. A series of checkpoints in the form of due dates for various phases of the project is essential to good management and motivation. One long paper may often constitute a major part of the term's grade and raise anxieties much more than several shorter papers or intermediate phases. These provide feedback and the chance to improve skills in analyzing, synthesizing, organizing, and writing. The one-shot approach—often loosely guided or even largely unguided—provides few opportunities for continued growth. A long paper should be segmented, with each part being evaluated separately, so that the students can use the constructive criticism to improve their performance as they go along and get a sense of one part being built upon the one before it.

The requirements as to the types and number of references to be used and the weighting for scoring purposes of each segment of the paper should be decided on, written out, and shared with the students at the outset. Very little guesswork remains under these conditions.

SCORING SHEET AS TEACHER/LEARNER AID. A scoring sheet which identifies the specifics being looked for and indicates their relative importance assists both the teacher and the student. When a scoring sheet such as that found below is used, all expectations are clearcut, and uncertainties are reduced. Because this also helps to spotlight goals, students are better able to produce effective end products. The scoring sheet is in itself a learning device and can be used as a department standard. It allows individual teachers to change percentage weights and due dates to fit individual class needs.

When a search paper is based upon the use of types of references for both content notes and bibliography, a measure of security for the student as well as control for the teacher is provided. A workable timetable can be developed and followed, coordinated with the use of an attack outline and a thesis statement. As each phase of the assignment becomes due, that much of the project is scored and recorded by the classroom teacher. The project based upon the Shakespeare play *Macbeth* (see page 118-120) is an example of this type of planning.

By making the search approach through the use of types of references, the classroom teacher can easily adapt the assignment to the abilities of students. While an able class may be asked to incorporate twenty references in a fifteen-page paper, another class may be asked for only fifteen references in a ten-page report. Classes that have great difficulty can be started with using only two or three references for reports of only two or three pages. For them, a series of short papers, each based upon one or two types of references can gradually introduce the range of types of references available. Ultimately, a longer paper requiring the use of a variety of types of references becomes an assignment they can handle.

The same approach can be used for oral reports. The only difference is that the students speak from their content note cards rather than write from them. Some caution, however, should be used in making an assignment based upon oral presentation. Much class time is given to this type of project, and usually, unless the classroom teacher makes it clear that there will be a test covering these oral reports, many students will fail to pay close attention. An approach which provides for sharing information in a limited time is to have students present a precis of their reports rather than reading or reporting on the entire paper.

SAMPLE PROJECT SCORING SHEET

I. Preliminary Planning (_____ % of final grade/date due _____)   Grade _____
    Attack outline approved _____
        Topic suitable _____   Limitations adequate _____
        Proper form used _____   Thesis statement accepted _____

II. Technical Processes (_____ % of final grade)
    Tentative bibliography cards (_____ % of final grade/date due _____)   Grade _____
        Form of entry follows style sheet _____   Call numbers given _____
        Numbered sequentially _____   Minimum number provided _____
        Required references represented _____
    Content cards approved (_____ % of final grade/date due _____)   Grade _____
        Keyed to tentative bibliography cards _____   Keyed to outline _____
        Single idea per card _____   Source paging given _____
        Representative of required references _____

III. Writing of the paper (_____ % of final grade/date due _____)   Grade _____
     Followed style sheet _____
        Abbreviations spelled out _____   Footnotes in correct style sheet form _____
        Bibliography in correct style sheet form _____ Text of paper in correct style sheet form _____
        Cover sheet in correct style sheet form _____
     Sources acknowledged _____
        Direct quotations _____   Indirect use of ideas _____

                                                          FINAL GRADE _____

N.B.: Should there be any questions regarding a source used or reference given in this paper, the student will have the opportunity to present proof before the final grade is given. Any evidence of plagiarism will result in a failing final grade. Failure to present material on due dates will result in reduction in credit of five points per day late.

3. Choosing a Topic

The initial step in the organization of a search project is of course the selection of the topic. Providing varying degrees of choice for a student in this matter is possible. The classroom teacher may assign a given topic to each student individually, allow students to choose from a selected list of topics, or permit students to choose their own topics with little or no guidance. This latter course of action is not recommended because few students have sufficient grasp of the course content at the beginning of the school year or the term to make wise choices of related topics. There is so little time to cover the content of any course that to allow students to work randomly outside of the course content is unwise. Also, students given this complete freedom of choice will tend to choose topics with which they already are familiar and thereby lose some of the benefits of the search project.

Classroom teachers who make sure that topics are either assigned to students or are selected from an approved list or group of topics associated with the course content will be helping both the students and themselves. Examples of activities in which the students are assigned a topic by chance are given on pages 90 and 115, such as: the drawing of titles of specialized dictionaries, and the drawing of pictures from the portrait file (face down,) for a freshman English assignment on the elderly.

Examples of activities using topic lists are found on pages 118, 121, 123, 144, 148-157, 168, and 173.

Few students will gravitate toward a topic about which they know little or nothing at the start. However, when everyone in the class has a new or unfamiliar topic assigned, the situation is viewed as fair though difficult by most students. The idea that choosing and working with a topic that is completely new may yield a higher mark than would a well worn one will seem strange to them at first; yet when it is explained, students usually understand it as a good possibility—albeit without any guarantees. It should seem logical to students that boredom with a subject they have used before is bound to show up in their written work, and that the teacher is going to react to dullness less favorably than to the freshness and enthusiasm that is evident when a student is making discoveries. Once students are pushed—and they often have to be pushed—into working with an unfamiliar topic, they are usually extra proud of their accomplishments when they are finished and pleased to have learned about something new. The ultimate realization does little, however, to reduce the complaints at the beginning or while the assignment is in progress. Peer expectation seems to call for continuous wails of overwork and "hard" teachers. Classroom teachers should not allow this clatter to dissuade them from pursuing the goal, however; and strong backing from library media teachers will help them to stand their ground.

Students will need to be carefully prepared and shown how to start digging for information with which they are essentially unfamiliar. Too often students know only how to outline from materials already constructed, and the concept that one organizes questions about an unknown topic in order to plan a search attack may be entirely new to them. They will need some help in how to think about, define, and delimit a topic before they even start to select one.

If a chosen topic were bridges, for example, this could mean that the paper would include information about all bridges during all times in all countries and of every type of construction. Similarly, if the topic were a poet, such as Wordsworth, this could mean that all of the poet's works might be expected to be discussed and evaluated. It is obvious that without limiting them in some way, these are not appropriate topics for five-, ten-, or even fifteen-page papers.

In the case of the topic, bridges, limiting by country would help. Limiting by type, such as cantilevered or suspension within that country, would help even more. Further limitation could be achieved by choosing a time period. A single bridge might be sufficient for the exercise at hand. In the case of Wordsworth, the choice of one or two poems that exemplified his work as a nature poet would suffice. These poems could either be compared or contrasted.

Sources of Ideas for Topics and Thesis Statements

Classroom teachers looking for ideas for topics to assign to students or students searching for a suitable topic when the classroom teacher has instructed them to "write on anything you wish" will find the use of specialized dictionaries and handbooks invaluable. These are helpful for choosing a topic for the same reasons that they should be the first reference stop once work on the paper has begun.

SPECIALIZED DICTIONARIES AND HANDBOOKS. The entries are short and to the point. They include the basic presearch information that provides leads to indexes or specialized references. Dates, geographic locations, names of colleagues or associates, and identification of the subject's outstanding works or contributions are usually included. The young student does not have the needed background to recognize the most important points made in a lengthy treatise, nor does the student have the time required to work through extensive material when the assignment deadline is short, even if the expertise were there.

Assistance is provided when the user of these tools recognizes that additional information is available in paragraphs under the terms that appear in small capitals (as opposed to italics), under *see* references, and under those indicated by *q.v.* Often a topic is fully treated only by checking several entries since the different aspects of it are given under each topic heading. Cross references should command full attention.

Using the two-paragraph entry on muckrakers from Benet's *Reader's Encyclopedia* as an example, the student could glean the following clues for further search:

1. The term is applied in both social studies and literature contexts.
2. Theodore Roosevelt is credited with coining the term and using it in a pejorative sense. Some references to Roosevelt could produce usable information (*e.g.*, biographies, autobiographies, and works on his presidency).
3. Roosevelt was familiar with *Pilgrim's Progress* from which he took the allusion. The student should read the portion of *Pilgrim's Progress* that contains the character who was so busy raking in the mud (muck) that he could not see the celestial crown above his head.
4. Muckraking was at its height between 1900 and 1910. Thus, the student is provided with a time span within which to concentrate his search.
5. *McClure's Magazine*, *Collier's* and *Cosmopolitan* took the lead in the movement. These periodicals are available on microform in many libraries, so students might be able to use them as primary resources through interlibrary cooperation
6. Authors whose articles appeared in these periodicals, some of whom based influential books upon them, include Ida Tarbell, Lincoln Steffens, and Samuel Hopkins Adams.

Biographies, autobiographies, and criticism of the writing of these authors should be useful. Books on political corruption and social injustice would include references, and books on women would include Tarbell.

7. Book titles lead the searcher to city politics; the U.S. Senate; and the oil, life insurance, and railroad industries, all of which provide additional leads.

8. In the field of fiction, Upton Sinclair's *The Jungle* is noted for its portrayal of the scandals in the meat-packing industry.

By using the short handbook article, the student is provided with the who, the what, and the when information needed to start finding out the where, the why, and the how aspects required to make a full report on the topic.

By using the entry from Benet for a person, Rupert Brooke, one can find the following clues:

1. Brooke was English and his dates were 1887–1915.

2. His writing format was poetry.

3. He was considered a Georgian poet as well as a war poet.

4. Outstanding titles include the sonnets called "1914", "Grantchester," and "The Great Lover."

5. Early work expressed idealized patriotism.

6. Later work was influenced (as T.S. Eliot's) by the study of 17th century poetry.

7. John Webster was the subject of a study done by Brooke.

8. Titles of poems of note in his later style were "Heaven" and "Dust."

9. The hero of St. John Ervine's novel *Changing Winds* is said to be based upon Brooke.

One is referred to the entry *Georgian*, where the information includes the following:

1. Group of English poets.

2. Their style dominated the early twentieth century.

3. They wrote of nature and rustic life in the manner of Wordsworth.

4. John Masefield's *The Everlasting Mercy* launched the movement, along with A. E. Houseman's *Shropshire Ballads*.

5. Publisher Edward Marsh pushed the movement along.

6. Named Georgian because King George V became King in 1910.

7. Fourteen poets are named as members of the movement, Brooke being one of them.

Another option is to use the title of a work, in this instance *The Moonstone.*

1. The novel was written in 1868 by Wilkie Collins. (See also Collins, Wilkie.)
2. A thumbnail sketch is given of the plot.
3. Sergeant Cuff, who solves the mystery, is probably the first detective in English fiction; and, therefore, the book starts the detective story genre.
4. The story is a mystery and detective story. There will be information on the genre. (In this case *detective story* does not appear in Benet's *Reader's Encyclopedia* but it does appear in Benet's *Reader's Encyclopedia of American Literature* and in other literary handbooks).

By using the cross reference made to Wilkie Collins, one learns, additionally, the following:

1. Collins was a good friend of Charles Dickens.
2. Both writers influenced one another.
3. Collins, the lesser of the two writers, did at times rival Dickens in description and character development and frequently excelled him in plot development.
4. Other Collins mystery stories include *Woman in White* (1860), *The New Magdalen* (1873), *The Haunted Hotel* (1879), and *Heart and Science* (1883).

Possible topics that could grow out of this paragraph might be the following:

1. Wilkie Collins, the first writer of English detective stories
2. The development of the English detective story: Collins, Doyle, Fleming
3. Similarities in the writing of Collins and Dickens

LITERARY CRITICISM. When the assignment involves literary criticism, one approach the student will find helpful is to read some excerpts of literary criticisms found in such titles as *Library of Literary Criticism* or the numerous volumes of *Contemporary Literary Criticism* (*CLC*). When a thought seems surprising, challenging, or unacceptable to the reader, it is possible to use that quotation as the base upon which to build a critical paper. The paper may be planned either to support the statement or to refute it.

A typical example is the excerpt from a critique in Volume 15, pages 412–413, of *CLC*:

Mrs. May, the central character in Flannery O'Connor's

1956 story, "Greenleaf," is obsessed equally with money and class status. She is disgusted with her "white trash" help, the Greenleafs, but they are a special source of vexation for her in that they have hardworking twin sons who have been successful in life, unlike her own boys.

This statement, made by critic Kathleen Rout, could provide the basis for a paper proving its correctness through citations from the short story.

Again, regarding Flannery O'Connor in a criticism by Caroline Gordon in the same volume of *CLC*, page 412:

She has written four short stories, "A Good Man is Hard to Find," "Good Country People," "The Displaced Person," and "The River," which seem to me nearly to approach perfection.... All her work is based upon the same architectural principle. This principle... is, I think, the fact that any good story, no matter when it was written or in what language, or what its ostensible subject matter, shows both natural and supernatural grace operating in the lives of human beings.

One or two of the stories mentioned could be examined to find evidence of the "natural and supernatural grace" referred to by Gordon.

Frederick J. Hoffman, speaking of William Styron (page 524, *CLC*) says: "He is, above all, concerned with the basic and timeless issue.... It is, in brief, the problem of believing, the desperate necessity for having the 'courage to be'."

All these are examples of thoughts the student might explore successfully.

SUBDIVIDED AND ANNOTATED TABLES OF CONTENTS. If the topic were to be in the area of American fiction, a wealth of topic ideas could be found in the table of contents of *American Fiction: An Historical and Critical Survey* by Arthur Hobson Quinn. Each chapter is followed by a combination of annotation and subtopic listings which outline the contents of that chapter in such a way that each segment is a possible paper topic. Chapter twenty-two, "The Romance of History and Politics," includes the following subtopics: the nature of the historical novel; the persistence of the type; Lew Wallace's romances of foreign life; Jane G. Austin's novels of colonial New England; Mary Hartwell Catherwood's stories of early

Canada; the historians turn to politics; Henry Adam's *Democracy* and John Hay's *Breadwinner*; Mrs. Burnett's *Through One Administration*; Edward Bellamy's romances of the past and future; the historical novel becomes a vogue; James Maurice Thompson; Paul Leicester Ford's political and historical fiction; Winston Churchill's historical novels; leading to his critical studies of political corruption; Mary Johnston's treatment of colonial Virginia and the Civil War; Owen Wister's celebration of the passing of the cowboy; the mass of second-rate fiction at the turn of the century; the steady continuation of the impulse during the twentieth century; Caroline Dale Snedeker's novels of Greek life; John T. McIntyre's novels of Philadelphia. Here is a wealth of ideas, any of which could serve as the base for building a successful search paper.

A similar approach can be used for history and social studies. The table of contents for Will Durant's *The Story of Civilization* includes subdivisions for material covered in each chapter. *The Reformation*, volume six, chapter two, includes "England," subtopics for the government, John Wyclif, the Great Revolt, the new literature, Geoffrey Chaucer, and Richard II. Chapter thirty-seven on science in the Age of Copernicus, can be used for science papers as well as for social studies. Subheads include the cult of the occult, the Copernican revolution, Magellan and the discovery of the earth, the resurrection of biology, Vesalius, the rise of surgery, Paracelsus and the doctors, the skeptics, and Ramus and the philosophers.

MULTIVOLUME REFERENCES. Another approach is to leaf through several volumes of a multivolume history which is designed to give a fairly simple overview of historical periods and events, and to observe the topic headings. One good example is the *Milestones of History* set published by Newsweek Books. Here are topics that could easily be developed into papers of worth, including: the gift of the Nile; the first law code; building the Great Wall of China; Hannibal challenges Rome; and Arminius, liberator of Germany. Since the set is arranged chronologically, one has only to select the volume that covers the time frame of interest. The proper dates and the topics are there.

CHRONOLOGIES PROVIDE IDEAS. Using a chronology can be a very helpful idea stimulator for projects. A book such as *The Timetables of History* by Bernard Grun is a delight. It is arranged in columns labeled history, politics; literature, theatre; religion, philosophy and learning; visual arts; music; science, technology, growth; daily life. The dates are given in the margins. Using the year 1550 and the heading visual arts, one finds: Benvenuto Cellini, *Perseus*, sculpture, Florence; beginning of early Baroque; beginnings of Japanese Ukiyoe painting; Lorenzo Lotto, *Nobleman in his Study*; Michelangelo, *Deposition from the Cross*, painting; Palladio, *Palazzo Chiericati and Villa Rotunda, Vicenza*; Titian, *Portrait of His Daughter Lavinia*; Giorgio Vasari, *Lives of the Artists*.

Under the year 1795 and the topic history and politics in the same book, one finds: bread riots and the White Terror in Paris; third French constitution enacted vesting power in the Directory; Napoleon appointed Commander in Chief, Italy; secret treaty between Austria and Russia for third partition of Poland (joined by Prussia); third partition of Poland; King Stanislas II abdicates; the Dutch surrender Ceylon to the British; Warren Hastings acquitted of high treason; Luxembourg capitulates to France; French occupy Mannheim and Belgium; Austria signs armistice with French; British forces occupy Cape of Good Hope; Treaty of San Lorenzo between the United States and Spain settles boundary with Florida and gives the United States right to navigate the Mississippi; Frederick William IV of Prussia born (d. 1861.)

Other useful chronologies are the three volumes by R. L. Storey titled *Chronology of the Medieval World, 800–1491, Chronology of the Expanding World, 1492–1762*, and *Chronology of the Modern World, 1763 to the Present Day* [1965] and William L. Langer's *An Encyclopedia of World History*. The latter is the most detailed and descriptive, but its coverage is largely limited to historical events with very little about the world of science: science and learning, 1450–1700; science and society, 1700–1800 (each of these with a six-page entry); and science and society since 1800, with a sixteen-page entry.

The Storey chronologies use an arrangement in which the events are listed on one page and topics on the other. Topic headings include economics, science, technology and discovery, religion and education, literature, philosophy, scholarship, and births and deaths.

PERIODICALS. Periodicals and journals, proliferating in ever more highly specialized areas, provide a fine resource both for choosing a topic and for preparing the search project based upon it when the time comes.

The field of mathematics lends itself to searching in the library media center. Magazines that contain regular columns of recreational mathematics will attract the interest of some students. Assignments can be made which will call for the use of periodicals for reporting current mathematical interests and information. There are always the biographical approaches, too, for learning more about the life and work of both modern and historical mathematicians.

4. Preparing for the Search

Successful development and completion of the search project depends upon students having first been taught how to think about assignment topics and how to use the library media center's materials. Nothing is as destructive to the motivation to learn as a search project that is poorly prepared for. It continually runs into dead ends and stone walls, and wastes hours of time. Search can be and should be an interesting and highly satisfying experience in self-direction and independent learning for the student who has been given adequate preparatory skills and the opportunity to practice them before being expected to produce.

Seeing to it that students are properly equipped to start a search project is a major contribution to not only the success of that particular project but to the student's whole academic career and later work life. The process being undertaken and learned now will have abiding value. It is the responsibility of the classroom teacher, teamed with the library media teachers, to insure that preparation for the undertaking all but guarantees its success.

This is a two-step process for the classroom teacher. He or she must be in confident command of the basic information needed to use the library media center's resources. The classroom teacher must also be certain that students have both the general background information and the specialized skills they will need to use the library media center effectively. In addition, the classroom teacher must be sure the students know how to apply this knowledge. This is the groundwork necessary before students are sent to the library media center to begin their specific search activity.

We have said that in initial planning the classroom teacher verifies that there is adequate material in the library media center's collection—or at least easily available to it—to support all of the topics from which students are to choose assignments. The wise classroom teacher also personally checks out a couple of examples and follows them through the indexing to see where possible problems may arise later for students. The classroom teacher is, after all, the source of the students' confidence; when that teacher is perceived to be floundering in the very processes they are expected to be able to master, it undermines belief in their own abilities. The classroom teacher should have used the machinery (for microforms, for example) in advance and become competent in its operation. When the classroom teacher can be at reasonable ease using the bibliographic tools, operating the equipment, and finding the locations of materials, the progress of a class is increased considerably.

General Understanding and Information

Presearch orientation is linked largely to the organization of information. There is some background information and language proficiency to be reviewed even before any specialized search skills are emphasized. For instance, because many references are arranged alphabetically, correct spelling of topics is absolutely essential. If there are alternative spellings for some words, this should be noted as well. The importance of accurate spelling should be discussed and students made aware that they must verify spellings before they set out on a reference search. There should be some discussion in the classroom of optional terminology, such as the fact that *water ballet* may be found under *synchronized swimming* or *oil* under *petroleum*. This is really a matter of vocabulary and of learning to think about words and their meanings and about possible relationships and synonyms. The logic of reference book organization should be explored and discussed—the fact that they can be organized either alphabetically; chronologically; or by theme, discipline, or geographic area.

Classroom teachers should prepare students to work effectively so that they can be assisted productively by the library media staff. For instance, a mumbled or mispronounced term is easily misunderstood by the library media teacher who is trying to help the student with references, and much valuable time is wasted. The importance of speaking clearly and pronouncing properly should be stressed as a presearch necessity. Reference librarians and library media teachers spend substantial amounts of time in their training and on the job trying to improve the "reference interview," which is the process of finding out what information the searcher really wants and relating it to available reference sources. The more precisely and specifically searchers can state requests and context, the better help they will get.

It is important to review with students such things as copyright dates; the word "modern" in a title can be misleading so copyright dates should always be checked. The word "contemporary" can also be misleading; students are inclined to think that it means invariably present day, at the same time as ourselves, when of course everyone had contemporaries in their own day, including Caesar and Jefferson.

A discussion of topics and how to choose them must precede the start of work in the library media center on the actual project itself. There should be class visits there beforehand both to learn specific skills and to look for and select a topic. The topic should be chosen and the attack outline completed by all students and approved by the classroom teacher before anyone may begin work on the search itself in the library media center. This means that the classroom teacher will know for certain that students know the date spans, the geographic areas, and the disciplines in which the topic falls that they have selected as the basis for their project. In this way, the library media teacher will be able to accurately deduce both the specific information the student needs and the classroom teacher's overall intent and learning objectives for each student as a product of the search.

Specific Bibliographic Skills

The classroom teacher must ascertain just what the gaps are both in the students' specific bibliographic skills and in their understanding of how to apply them. It is easy to assume that students of upper elementary, middle school, and high school have learned how to use a library somewhere, from someone, sometime. But exactly what they know and how well they can apply it will largely decide the success or failure of the search learning experience and therefore, cannot be left to chance or assumption. Of course, when asked if they know how to use the library media center, students will raise a resounding affirmative chorus. However, many students will have a limited view of how to use the center and of what they need to know how to do in it.

DIAGNOSTIC TESTING. For finding out what students do know and what further help they need, the diagnostic test can be very useful both to the student and to the teacher. The information which the test indicates has truly been learned will not need to be repeated. When tests show that students can apply the needed skills, they can go ahead. Others will be required to do remedial work before proceeding with assigned projects. When students realize that attentiveness to the routine instruction in the library media center "pays off", attention improves.

Diagnostic testing is not perfect despite its many merits. Frequently, students who have been exposed to library skills instruction in lower grades can recite correct answers or fill in blanks on a paper and pencil test without being able actually to apply the information they appear to have mastered. They know that fiction is arranged alphabetically by author, but they cannot go from the catalog to the shelves and apply that information. They may know that there are author, title, and subject entries in the catalog, but they often cannot differentiate among those categories or use them properly. The classroom teacher is wise to look for demonstrated, hands-on skills before structuring search assignments.

PERFORMANCE-BASED TESTS. To determine how well students can apply bibliographic knowledge, a performance-based test may be given on site in the library media center. Here, students could be supplied with a card asking them to find several different types of materials from the codes given in the card catalog. If all of the items for each student come from a single file drawer, no one will get in anyone else's way. Cards of exercises can be used another time, so answers should not be marked on them but on a separate sheet of paper.

Samples of exercises that might be used to insure the ability to find material using various access points in the card catalog (all from the "P" drawer) follow.

For each exercise below complete these steps:
1. Find the author and title of a biography of Edgar Allen Poe.
    (a) Write down the author's last name, title of the book, and call number on your paper.
    (b) Go to the shelf and find the book which you will take to your teacher to be checked off.
    (c) Replace the book on the shelf where it belongs.
    (d) If the book is not on the shelf, ask the teacher to come with you so that you can indicate where the book would be found if it were on the shelf.
2. Find a book of fiction by Alexander Perry.
3. Locate the book *Pioneer Forts* by James Sill. (Note: the title chosen for #3 should be a reference book.)
4. Locate a book about pyramids that is *not* a reference book.

Students may go to an incorrect area to locate a book and therefore find that the book is "not there." The teacher's being along to concur that the book is not in place makes it possible for the teacher to identify the problem the student is having and to give instruction to alter the mistaken procedure.

Once the tests and demonstrations have identified gaps to be filled and the extent of review needed, this help can be provided by the classroom teacher and the library media teacher in both classroom and center sites. Instruction in basics (some areas included in the next chapter) should be followed by practice sessions in the center.

Class Visit to the Library Media Center

The first visit of a classroom group to the library media center in anticipation of the search project can be a difficult occasion even when good preparations have been made for it. Both the classroom teacher and the library media teacher must anticipate the problems that will surely arise, one of them being that student uncertainties will demand greater than usual time and attention from both teachers working in close cooperation. It should be made clear to the students that both types of teachers are working together as an instructional team.

The classroom teacher who is used to having the class within the boundaries of a classroom can feel out of control during the experience of having students scattered throughout a library media center. Having an assigned area as a base of operations to which students report at intervals is helpful—a necessity even—but this alone does not take care of the problem. The students must be able to move about, leaving and returning to this base as they explore indexes, locate materials in various formats (recordings, filmstrips, microforms) or use microform and computer equipment.

Students will seem to need assistance all at once. Even if the things they are expected to follow up have been made clear to them before leaving their classroom, they will still need to be reassured that they are doing what they are supposed to be doing. It is inevitable that they will find exceptions to the indexing, variations from what they have learned in the instructional sessions. All will want individual attention.

Two things help a great deal: the fact that the library media teacher is there to assist, working side by side with their classroom teacher, and the fact that the classroom teacher is in full and confident command of card catalog, indexes, and the location of media in various formats. When a classroom teacher is launching a search project with a class, that class must have top priority attention from the library media center staff. Once the students have got themselves well into their projects and are on their third or fourth visits to the school library media center, the situation will be markedly different. On the first, preparatory visit, it is very important that the students and their classroom teacher feel fully supported and on their way to a successful experience with their search projects.

A class should not be scheduled into the library media center for too many consecutive days. Following two days in the center, the third day should at least be started in the classroom to evaluate and take stock. It may be found that only a few members of the class need additional time in the library media center for instructional purposes, and they may be sent to the center while the remainder of the class works in the classroom. Too much time spent in the library media center in one unbroken span leads to wasting time, and the false impression by students that they need not extend themselves since there is going to be "plenty of time" to get the job done. Students, especially beginners, rarely estimate correctly the amount of time they will need to organize and complete the search project.

Indeed, the classroom teacher who is experiencing an initial search project assignment may also underestimate the amount of time that will be required for students to do the project rigorously and effectively. It does not matter so much what age the students are—upper elementary through high school—as it does that this is their first experience with the search assignment format. Once students have been led through the entire process, the repeat experiences are much smoother. The classroom teacher should plan for a bit of slippage in the initial time schedule. Even when teachers have checked the school calendar in advance for scheduled interruptions such as holidays, test periods, pep rallies, fire drills, and auditorium programs, there will always be unexpected disruptions that will extend the time needed to complete a lengthy search project.

5. Reviewing Basic Skills

Observing students at work in a library media center confirms that it is the lack of basic information and basic skills that often causes them to fail to locate materials they need. A review of the basics prior to beginning a search project is recommended. The areas discussed below are especially troublesome and should be emphasized.

Two Ways To Alphabetize

One of the things that trips students up is that there are two ways to alphabetize. Most of them probably learned letter-by-letter alphabetizing during dictionary study in elementary school because dictionaries are arranged using the letter-by-letter system.

However, if students are to use the card catalog (or book, fiche or computerized catalogs for that matter), they will need to understand and be able to master word-by-word alphabetizing because this is the system that is generally used for catalogs in the library media center. According to this system, the first word is placed in relationship to another first word. The student learns to stop after the first word, applying the "nothing comes before something" concept. Only when first words are identical does one consider the next word for placement. Within each word unit, however, the alphabetizing is done letter-by-letter.

Example of letter-by-letter: *Newark, Newell, New York, New Zealand*
Example of word-by-word: *New York, New Zealand, Newark, Newell*

If dictionaries use letter-by-letter alphabetizing and catalogs use word-by-word alphabetizing, which systems do handbooks, encyclopedias, and other specialized references that are arranged alphabetically use? One discovers that it depends entirely upon the preference of the author or indexer. Some use one; some use the other.

The importance of being aware of the two systems of alphabetizing lies in the fact that as the size of the index one is using increases,

35

the problems which will arise from trying to apply the wrong alphabetic system also increase. Students do not need to try to memorize which reference uses which system, but they should be alert to the fact that they may be misapplying a system of alphabetizing if they do not find an entry where they believe it ought to be. They should learn automatically to verify that they are using the correct approach. Otherwise, students may miss finding the information they require.

When in doubt about which system is operative for a particular reference source, there is a short cut to finding out which system is being dealt with. Students can turn to sections of the index where a short word such as *new*, *old*, or *I* is likely to be used repeatedly. Rapid scanning shows whether all of the entries with *new* are together first, which would mean the word-by-word system is operating, or whether the words *new* are interspersed with other words beginning with the letters *n e w*, which would mean the letter-by-letter system.

Example of word-by-word: New Amsterdam, New Bedford, New England, New York, New Zealand, Newark, Newbery, Newmarket

Example of letter-by-letter: New Amsterdam, Newark, New Bedford, Newbery, New England, Newmarket, New York, New Zealand

In indexes such as those for general encyclopedias, this scanning may call for examination of several pages to make sure. The larger the index, the more difference the system makes. The user can be off only a few entries, or the error may be as large as several columns or pages or, in the case of a large card catalog, several drawers.

Card Catalog Subject File

Dividers that stick up above the cards in the card catalog drawers with topics printed on them are guides, similar to key words at the tops of pages in alphabetized references. Just because there is no divider sticking up with a needed topic printed on it does not mean that the subject is not in the drawer. Many other subjects are filed between the key topics on dividers.

Does no subject entry mean there is no information in the catalog? No, but this is a common misconception. Students need to be made aware that there may indeed be material about a subject in the catalog even though the subject does not appear as a separate entry. A subject entry will be used in a catalog only when there is a whole book, kit, tape, or other format unit (or a substantial part of one) devoted to that subject in the center. Much, much more information on a subject can be found through indexes of specialized references in the field, periodical indexes, newspaper indexes, collected biographies, and the like. Those early author, title, and subject drills that students had in elementary school were fine for a beginning but there is much more information available in small segments, listed under more encompassing terms, or even under more specialized terms than just what is to be found in whole books on a subject.

Teachers who give students practice in switching terminology from general to more specific terms and back again do them a great service. Attention should be called to subject heading tools such as *Sears List of Subject Headings* or the *Library of Congress Subject Headings* (whichever is used in the catalog at hand) and tools such as *Subject Cross Reference Index*, which gives significant assistance in forming proper terminology to use when locating coverage of topics through the use of the *Reader's Guide to Periodical Literature*.

Data on the Book Spine

When using a subject entry it is important to verify the call number (all of it), the author, and the title. A great number of students will go to the shelf expecting to find the subject terminology printed on the spine of the book they want. It may not be; but the title, call number, and author's name will be. BIOLOGY may be the subject of the book, and BIOLOGY will appear as a subject heading on the catalog card but not necessarily on the book's spine.

Example of book spine:
Cells:
Plant and
Animal [title]
574.2 [call number]
Smith [author]

Example of card entry:
          BIOLOGY
574.2   Smith, Susan.
          Cells: Plant and animal /
          by Susan Smith. — 5th ed. —
          Philadelphia : Oakum Press, 1981.

Location and Format Clues

A location or format clue preceding a call number in the upper left hand corner of the catalog card is worth noticing. Examples of these clues are REF. indicating a reference book, TR(C) indicating a cassette tape recording, PRINT indicating a large picture, or FICHE for microfiche. These clues not only tell the user what format the material is in but also gives guidance about where to find it. Many students seem to be unsure of finding these materials and sidestep use of them. It will help a great deal if the classroom teacher will clearly express approval of nonprint resources as references and also be certain that students know their location, understand their use, and know how to identify them bibliographically. A few pertinent frames of a filmstrip, or a few minutes from a tape or phonodisc can add greatly to a student's comprehension of a fact or idea.

It is essential that students appreciate that using footnoting for these extracts from nonprint materials is little different from using it for a few pages from a periodical or a chapter from a book. But there are some differences and substitutions, and students must know what they are. There are titles, authors, publishers, and copyright dates for all materials regardless of format, but number of frames or playing time is to be used in place of page numbers. A few minutes of instruction and discussion about this by the teacher will legitimatize it and provide needed confidence for the students.

Scope and Purpose of the Reference Tool

Bibliographic information and notes appearing on a catalog card help the user determine whether a reference will be useful or not because they indicate the scope and purpose of the reference tool. In the specialized references there have to be some limitations imposed upon the contents. It is important to learn what these limitations are and pay attention to them when looking for information. For instance, many students will look for biographical information about a famous living American in the *Dictionary of American Biography*. They need to know that the reference contains only names of deceased people. Also, recently deceased persons would not be included until a supplement covering the year of their death is printed.

Similarly, collected biographical references will give attention not only to date span, but to geographic areas and to professions. The Kunitz author references are a case in point. Titles in the series include: *European Authors, 1100–1900, British Authors before 1800, British Authors of the Nineteenth Century, Twentieth*

Century Authors, and *World Authors 1950–1970.* Here profession, geographic area, and dates are important parts of the volume titles.

ALA Filing Rules

The card catalog is filed according to ALA Filing Rules. Filing rules vary to some extent depending upon profession. Students in office practice courses find that they learn rules which differ from those applied to catalogs in library media centers. To further complicate things, there have been revisions made recently in the *ALA Filing Rules* used by catalog makers. These changes have been made necessary in part by the widespread and increasing use of computers in all areas of library work as in all other information-handling areas of life. Computers require absolute uniformity and logic. The latest of these changes was mandated with the publication of the 1980 American Library Association's *ALA Filing Rules.* This revision of filing rules was designed to coordinate with the application of the revision of the Anglo-American Cataloging Rules, an attempt to make catalog entries more universal in line with the computerized systems now used worldwide in information networks.

There is no way of knowing how rapidly all library media centers will adopt the 1980 rules. Many will not elect to do so either because of the labor and the costs involved or because they do not want to change the way they have been doing things. So students will have to become aware of problems in filing. Especially if they are having trouble finding the information they are seeking, students must be willing to ask for assistance and for verification that they are using the right approach in whatever facility they are using. Despite revisions of filing rules, many of the basics of the systems remain the same.

SYSTEM FOR THE CARD CATALOG. Students should remember that the catalog continues to apply word-by-word alphabetizing. The student who tries to find *To Kill A Mockingbird* under *tok* will not find it. It must be remembered that in a word-by-word alphabetizing system, the first word—in this case *To*—is what is considered. *To* will be far in front of *tok.*

CHANGES IN THE MAC RULE. *M', Mac,* or *Mc* at the start of names will usually create uncertainty. Traditionally, in card catalogs all three forms have been entered as if each was spelled *Mac.* This has allowed for looking in a single place in the catalog or index when the searcher was uncertain about the precise spelling of the word—a common situation if one has only heard the name spoken and not seen it in print.

Example: McBride, MacHenry, McIntyre, M'Leod, Macmillan

Other types of directories and indexes such as the telephone directory have made a practice of alphabetizing these entries according to their exact spellings. Cross references have been provided to remind the searcher of other possibilities should the desired information not be found at once.

The 1980 rules have attempted to simplify filing for the user as well as to make filing compatible with computerized processes. According to these new rules, the entries should be made according to precise spellings. Reference books that already exist are not likely to be changed, yet they will continue to be useful and used, requiring the searcher to be able to use either system.

CHANGES IN ABBREVIATIONS. Abbreviations have been filed in the past as if they were spelled out, but the new rules, following the spelling as is, change the filing of abbreviations drastically. The problem for the user and searcher will no longer be how to spell out the word the abbreviation stands for but to know exactly how the entry is cast, or written out.

Lt. Hornblower will no longer cause a spelling problem ("How do you spell lieutenant?") because it will be entered under *l t*. *Dr. Faustus* will be entered under *d r* while *The Doctor in Spite of Himself* will be entered under *d o*. Initials will be filed as individual words. Acronyms (initials without periods) will form single word units. For example:

I see red	IBM application program
I.T. & T.	Intelligent life
I.W.A.	Ion beams
I will wed	IQSY
IAMPA Symposia	Ivy Hall

The ampersand (&) will be filed as if spelled out in the language of the publication (*and* in English, *et* in French). For example:

A & B Company
A and P Company
Anklets, a horse
Art lines

For a long time, perhaps for the foreseeable future, the searcher will have to be aware of multiple possibilities and be ready to try them all or seek assistance.

CHANGES IN NUMERALS. According to the new filing rules, the number drawer(s) will precede the first alphabetic drawer. The entries will be in strict numeric sequence. Both superscript and subscript numbers will be filed as "on-the-line" numbers. Any superscript number will be filed as if it had a single space in front of it. Characters and punctuation are considered single spaces. It should be emphasized that the sequence of the numbers is according to the actual written sequence of individual numerals and not according to numerical value. For example, the following titles including numbers in the left-hand column would be considered as shown in the right-hand column for filing purposes.

1:00 a.m.	1 space 0
1^3 is 1	1 space 3
1/3 of a family	1 space 3
2 + and 3 −	2
2.5 percent	2 space 5
3 strikes is out	3
3.2 beer for all	3 space 2
3/3's	3 space 3
3/4 more	3 space 4
3:10 to Yuma	3 space 10

Within the same number phrase, alphabetizing by the word following the numerals will be traditional. For example:

2.5 percent
3 alphabets
3D sketches
3 M Company
3 point 2 and what goes with it
3.2 beer for all
3/3's

Roman numerals will be interfiled together with Arabic numerals. For example:

$10 a day [dollar sign is ignored]
X Roman holidays
10 ways to save.

The searcher must now be aware of the precise casting of the title in order to locate the title beginning with a numeral. Is the title *101 Best Poems*, in which case the entry would be placed in the first drawer of a file case, or is it *One Hundred One Best Poems*, in which case it would be in the "O" drawer? A searcher will no longer have to look in the "N" drawer under *Nineteen* for *1984* (or the "O" drawer for *One Thousand Nine Hundred Eighty-Four* if one did not know that dates were entered as they were said) because, according to the new rules, the title would be in the number drawer, right where the individual digits would place it: *1984*.

CHANGES IN COMPOUND WORDS AND NAMES. Compound words and names will, in most instances, be relocated with the application of the revised filing rules. Under the earlier rules, entries were placed according to the composition of a compound word or name. Compounds made up of a prefix and a word were considered as a single word unit whereas compounds consisting of a series of complete words were considered as separate words. By the revised rules, each part of a compound (and this includes prefixes) is considered a separate word to be filed word by word.

As a result, the searcher will now need to know whether a name such as Vandenberg is spelled Van den Berg, Vanden Berg, or Vandenberg. No longer will all three forms be filed together (based upon the old rule that prefixes would be run together as if they were a single word unit); they will be separated rather widely depending upon the precise spelling and the number of entries in the index. For example, the following could be a possible arrangement of the same entries by the new and the old systems:

New system	*Old system*
Van Den Berg, Alan	Van Den Berg, Alan
Van den Berg, Lawrence	Vandenberg, Arthur
Van den Bergh, Kas	Vanden Berg, Glen
Van Denburgh, John	Van den Berg, Lawrence
Van der Horst, Ulrich	Van den Bergh, Kas
Van Derveer, Lettie	Van Denburgh, John
Van Dyke, Henry	Van der Horst, Ulrich
Vanden Berg, Glen	Van Derveer, Lettie
Vandenberg, Arthur	Van Dyke, Henry

CHANGES IN SUBDIVISIONS. Subdivisions of topics, long a problem (even in a divided catalog which has separate sections for author, title, and subject entries), have been significantly affected by the change in filing rules. Basically, the punctuation which is used to indicate a subdivision, and which has been recognized as an influence upon alphabetic placement, is now ignored for filing purposes. The punctuation mark is considered a single space separating words, each of which will be addressed individually and in sequence within the word string. Whereas old style filing kept all entries of a given subject together with the subdivisions appearing in alphabetic order, the new method allows the subject to become separated by entries relating to other topics and functions. For example:

New style	*Old style*
WATER	WATER
WATER—ANALYSIS	WATER—ANALYSIS
WATER BALLET	WATER—FLUORIDATION
WATER BIRDS	WATER—POETRY
WATER COLOR PAINTING	WATER—POLLUTION
WATER COLORS	WATER—QUALITY
WATER—FLUORIDATION	WATER—STATISTICS
WATER—POETRY	WATER BALLET
WATER—POLLUTION	WATER BIRDS
WATER—QUALITY	WATER COLOR PAINTING
WATER SPORTS	WATER COLORS
WATER—STATISTICS	WATER SPORTS
WATER SUPPLY	WATER SUPPLY

In a dictionary catalog in which authors, titles, and subjects are all interfiled, the separation of entries for the same subject would be even greater. For example:

MEN
Men and boys
MEN—BIOGRAPHY
MEN—CIVIL RIGHTS
Men, David Ellis
MEN—EDUCATION
Men for freedom
Men from Mars
Men going workless
Men hating war
MEN—RESEARCH
MEN—STATISTICS
Mendel's Law
MEN'S CLOTHING

One subdivision application remains the same. When the subdivision HISTORY is further subdivided, its subdivisions will be entered chronologically. For example:

UNITED STATES
UNITED STATES—HISTORY
UNITED STATES—HISTORY—COLONIAL PERIOD,
   CA. 1600-1775
UNITED STATES—HISTORY—KING PHILIP'S WAR,
   1675-1676
UNITED STATES—HISTORY—QUEEN ANNE'S WAR,
   1702-1713
UNITED STATES—HISTORY—FRENCH AND INDIAN
   WAR, 1755-1763
UNITED STATES—HISTORY—REVOLUTION,
   1775-1783
UNITED STATES—HISTORY—WAR OF 1812
UNITED STATES—HISTORY—CIVIL WAR, 1860-1865
UNITED STATES—HISTORY—WAR OF 1898
UNITED STATES—HISTORY—20TH CENTURY
   [1900-1999]
UNITED STATES—HISTORY—1901-1953
UNITED STATES—HISTORY—1945-

Note that the century is begun with the decade year and will therefore be considered to include the years 1800 through 1899 or 1900 through 1999. Similarly, decades will be considered as 1970 through 1979 or 1980 through 1989.

EXCEPTIONS TO THE CHARACTER-BY-CHARACTER RULE. Although the basic rule is to follow through the word string character by character, there are the following exceptions:

1. Initial articles (*a*, *an*, *the*) will be ignored. This is true in any language. The articles will be respected for filing when they appear elsewhere. This is a continuation of established practice.
2. Character strings beginning with numerals are now placed in initial drawers before character strings beginning with letters. (This is new and has been discussed earlier.)
3. Relators used in name headings are ignored. These are terms showing the role of a person or corporate body in relation to a specific work. Terms such as those associated with legal documents such as *appellant, respondent, plaintiff* are

skipped. For example, *Standard Oil Company, respondent,* would simply be *Standard Oil Company* for filing purposes.

4. Terms of honor and address, when the access term begins with a surname, are ignored. For example:

Jenkins, Sir Andrew
Jenkins, Dame Bertha Mae
Jenkins, Cynthia
Jenkins, David John

Note that terms of honor and address, when the access term begins with a forename, are used. For example:

James, Abbott of Falls
James, Bishop of Nearshire
James, Duke of York

Note that explanatory entries such as *see* and *see also* entries are placed before the subject. There is no problem with *see* references as there are no other entries listed, and one is being told what heading to use instead of the one at hand. However, logic may suggest that *see also* references should come after the subject has run its course, but the filing rules call for the *see also* reference to come at the beginning of the topic.

By and About Rule

The "by and about" rule is used in many specialized indexes and references. In instances where persons are authors or creators of note, catalogs and indexes will carry entries both by and about the person. The "by and about" rule indicates that those entries referring to work by the person will precede those entries others have written about the person. Because subjects ("about" entries) are traditionally placed in all capital or boldface type, they are readily recognizable. Examples of each are:

By (lower case)	*About (all capitals)*
Cather, Willa	CATHER, WILLA
My Antonia	Jones, Robert
	Voice of the immigrant

It makes a lot of difference whether the searcher is looking for something someone has written or said in a speech, or whether the searcher needs materials about that person.

In the case of *Reader's Guide to Periodical Literature,* earlier volumes appeared to use the alphabet twice under a person's name, the first time for those articles by the person and the second time for the articles about the person. Later volumes include a subdivision separating the two types of information. The "by" entries still come first, but the word "about" now appears in the subdivision spacing where the content changes. The user of *Reader's Guide to Periodical Literature* still needs to know about the rule to use the earlier indexes effectively.

Essay and General Literature Index is another reference which is organized using the "by and about" rule. Here, too, in later volumes the word *about* is used as a guide.

The new, computerized catalog listing does not make the division for "by and about" but mixes the two together. In card catalogs which are divided according to author/title and subject, there is no trouble differentiating. However, in a dictionary-style catalog, the author and subject cards will be interfiled according to the information appearing on the *second* line. In the example above, *My Antonia* would come after Jones, Robert.

6. Organizing the Search Project

Choosing a Stylesheet

A variety of "how-to" manuals for creating a search paper are available, and these usually include examples of acceptable footnote and bibliography formats for print items. Fewer include examples for nonprint items, although there is at least one reference, *A Style Manual for Citing Microform and Nonprint Media* by Eugene B. Fleischer (American Library Association, 1978) which addresses this need.

When a stylesheet is accepted for use throughout the school in all departments, the students are able to practice the use of the agreed upon bibliographic forms until they really have learned them. This will be less confusing than changing form with each teacher and subject. Nevertheless, students should understand that there are a variety of stylesheets in use which are equally good. The important thing is consistency. Once a style has been decided upon, it should be used consistently throughout a paper.

To save time and to reduce the necessity for reworking information, the student should begin work on a search with a stylesheet in hand. If, from the very beginning, the information being taken down is recorded in complete and proper format, the work will need to be done only once.

Students should be advised to remember to verify which stylesheet has the approval of their college or individual professor when they go on to higher education. Usually an official designation will have been made either by the college or by a department.

Limiting the Topic

As the next step in planning the search project, the student must determine what will be included and what will be excluded from the paper. Deciding on areas to be omitted is very important because only partial coverage of a general topic can be developed within a short paper.

The planning and structuring of the final paper must take place before work is begun, and this is most likely to be done efficiently by asking questions of oneself. It is essential that the student understand that one does not have to have answers to the questions in order to plan the search. This is, in fact, probably the most difficult of concepts for the students and the most challenging aspect of instruction for the classroom teacher. Students who have had experience in outlining only materials that have already been written, such as their textbooks, find it incredibly difficult to take content that is not yet written and develop a logical outline. Students usually try to reject the entire approach until they have been led through the process. After having been given a bit of individual attention to work out these initial steps the first time, students often admit that it was much easier than they had thought it would be and laugh at themselves for having made a fuss about doing it.

As a preparatory or introductory exercise in organization, the teacher may want to use a list of related terms including one term that encompasses all of the others. Many of the elements required to do this exercise are also required to create an attack outline. For example, several acceptable outlines could be made from the terms included in the list which follows. Each would be correct, the differences reflecting individual preferences, although the relationships are the same in each variation.

List of Terms

coconut	Japanese maple	silver maple
date	maple	spruce
deciduous	Norway maple	trees
evergreen	oak	
fir	palm	
	pine	

Sample Outlines

No. 1	No. 2	No. 3
Trees	Trees	Trees
I. Palm	I. Evergreen	I. Deciduous
A. Date	A. Firs	A. Oaks
B. Coconut	B. Spruces	B. Maples
	C. Pines	1. Japanese
		2. Silver
		3. Norway

II. Evergreen	II. Deciduous	II. Palm
A. Pines	A. Maples	A. Date
B. Firs	1. Norway	B. Coconut
C. Spruces	2. Silver	
	3. Japanese	
	B. Oaks	
III. Deciduous	III. Palm	III. Evergreen
A. Oaks	A. Coconut	A. Pines
B. Maples	B. Date	B. Spruces
1. Silver		C. Firs
2. Norway		
3. Japanese		

As a further exercise leading toward the logical organization of the search paper, students might try the following. Assume that a paper will be developed with focus just on the Japanese maple tree. Using the "Five W's" formula (Who, What, When, Where, and Why/How) of the journalism profession, the searcher could develop questions to be used later in an attack outline. The attack outline will contain only the facts. The introductory, transitional, and summary sections, necessary parts of the finished paper, are not included. The attack outline is intended to aid in searching for information, and designed to help control and organize it once it is found.

In connection with areas of interest that are to be included in the paper and those to be excluded, we come to the questions mentioned earlier, such as the following:

Where does the tree grow in the U.S.?
Does the tree grow in Japan?
Is it native to Japan?
How did it get its name?
What is its Latin name?
When was it identified?
By whom?
Who brought it to U.S.?
What is it used for?
Is it grown in pots indoors?
How tall does it grow?
What are its special characteristics: leaf, flower, seed, root structure, size?
Was it more or less popular in earlier years? Why?

How is the tree propagated?
What pests attack the tree?
How long does the tree live?
How much does the tree cost if bought at a nursery?
Is it a popular tree? Why or why not?

Note again that at this point the answers to these questions are unknown. Anticipate that this state of no information will surely be troublesome to at least some students. They need to be kept assured that it will come out all right as they move along to the next steps.

Creating an Attack Outline

First of all, the relationship among the questions asked needs to be sorted out. Each element of the questioning formula may be used as an outline heading. For example, the "Who" questions might include "Who brought it to the U.S.?" and "Who identified it?" The "Where" questions might include "Does the tree grow in Japan?" and "Where does the tree grow in the U.S.?" as well as "Is it grown in pots indoors?" Among the "Why" questions would be such as "Why is the tree popular?" and "Was it more or less so in earlier years and why?"

The "When" questions may be used as subtopics for any of the other parts. One could, for example, ask a "When" question to the questions in the "Who" section and to the second "Why" question to yield subtopics for the outline. The remaining questions posed in the example all come under "What."

One makes a logical arrangement and sequence within and between categories. Just as in the outline examples given the order of categories of tree types made no difference, it will make no difference which of the "Five W's" comes first. Some students will be comfortable having the "What" first; others will wish to start with "Who"; or some even might find "Why" a good point of departure.

The "What" segment might begin to look as follows:

The Japanese Maple Tree
I. What
    A. Name
        1. Latin name
        2. How named
    B. Characteristics
        1. Height
        2. Bole size
        3. Rate of growth

4. Age
5. Leaves
   a) Size
   b) Shape
   c) Color
      1) Summer
      2) Fall
6. Flowers
   a) Size
   b) Shape
   c) Color
7. Seeds
   a) Size
   b) Shape
   c) Color
C. Natural enemies
D. Uses
E. Methods of propagation
   a) Seeds
   b) Cuttings
   c) Nursery stock and cost

The "Who", "Where", and "Why" segments will be given Roman numerals and will be much shorter.

An alternative method for devising questions to be answered and arranging them into an attack outline might be to tie them in with types of reference sources. Roman numerals could in this instance identify clusters of questions to be pursued in biographical, geographical, or historical reference sources.

For every topic there is a person involved: someone started it, developed it, makes it today, uses it, sells it. In some way a person is involved so biographical references can be applied. For every topic there is bound to be a geographical element, too: the author's area of residence while growing up or going to school; the history of the region or an area inhabited by an animal or plant—types of information that can be supplied by an atlas or gazeteer. There is need to consult a history of the topic in order to provide its proper historical setting. Almost everything is evaluated in some way, so a critical evaluation could be applied. Primary sources should be used to provide the first-hand accounts of a contemporary. Often a social history gives useful information concerning the times in which something existed, was used, or was popular. The chances are good that there will be a quotation of some sort that applies either to the exact topic or to the subject in general. Periodicals and newspapers can provide related articles.

All of these sources should be included in a thorough search, and may be required by the classroom teacher. Questions can be phrased to match this type of reference formula and the attack outline developed from them.

Students will want to know what they should do about information they discover while doing their search that they had not anticipated when making their attack outlines. The answer is that, although structure and planning are of great importance, modifications may be made to accommodate any element of significance found while searching the topic that does not fit into the proposed outline. On the other hand, students should be cautioned against grabbing at just anything of interest and trying to add it to the paper. Planning requires judicious exclusion as well as inclusion, and the paper that is based upon such a foundation will be superior to one that is not. If planning has been done thoroughly and thoughtfully, most additional material can be confidently put aside for the next paper or for someone else's.

Using a Card System

Students need to be shown an effective system for keeping track of progress when they are preparing a search paper. One of the simplest systems is based upon the use of three-by-five-inch index cards.

Making Tentative Bibliography Cards

The tentative bibliography cards list possible sources that one will wish to consult later. The information to be recorded on the bibliography card will be found in the card catalog, in bibliographies, and in special indexes such as those to periodicals and newspapers. There will be many more materials available than will be used, so the searcher should be as selective as possible. Content annotations, when available, should be used as guides.

At this point the student searcher needs to have the stylesheet, a pack of three-by-five-inch index cards, and a good pen in hand. Care should be taken to follow the prescribed form, to take down complete information, and to write carefully so that days later when the first draft of the paper or the final bibliography is being prepared, the student will not have to retrace steps to verify words or sources. All punctuation and spacing given in the stylesheet examples should be followed exactly, noting such things as the fact that articles in a periodical appear with quotation marks, while the title of the periodical itself (or a book,) will be underlined. Using ink avoids the smudging and blurring that is typically the fate of notes written in pencil.

When making the tentative bibliography cards, two coding steps save time: 1) number the cards in the upper right hand corner in sequential order (1, 2, 3...) and 2) place the library's call number in the upper left hand corner of the card. If the searcher uses more than one library, it is a good idea to indicate in which library the reference was found. If the call number is not noted at this time, the student will have to return to the catalog later to find the number because eventually the item will need to be located on the shelves. When the search project requires the use of specific types of references, it is useful to note at the bottom of the tentative bibliography card which type of reference this source is. An example of tentative bibliography cards:

B
L   Jones, Marvin   1
(H.S.)   *The Story of Robert E. Lee*
           New York: Macmillan, 1979

                                          (Biography)

Per.
           Allen, Susan   11
           "How Lee Grew"
           Time, Vol. 56, June 24, 1970, pp. 41–46

                                          (Periodical)

This coding process means that the bibliographic information on the tentative bibliography card identifies the reference yielding content information placed later on a note card. This practice eliminates having to copy the bibliographic information repeatedly onto every content card. By using this coding system, the bibliographic information will be copied only twice, once onto the tentative bibliography card and a second time onto the final bibliography if the source has actually provided content for the paper.

Up to this point, all of the student's work has been preparatory. Students who have been in the habit of going to a general encyclopedia and copying out information will probably be hard to convince that such preparatory work is necessary. However, establishing due dates, insisting that each step is fully performed, as well as grading each step as it is completed have proven to be effective means of keeping a class on schedule (see pages 19, 116, 119, and 123).

Taking Content Notes

Using the tentative bibliography cards, the student selects one reference to locate and examine for content. It makes good sense to start with a specialized handbook or dictionary article since information given in these short entries provides significant clues to other sources. Names of persons, movements, dates, and places all can be used to advantage in searching the indexes of specialized references. The second source to consult would logically be the specialized encyclopedia which will give depth and detail. The difference between the general and the specialized encyclopedias must be clearly understood before a classroom teacher directs students not to use a general encyclopedia for a particular project. The student may hear only the term encyclopedia and believe that the classroom teacher has eliminated any reference source containing that word in its title. This is not the intent when one is working with references by type. Specialized encyclopedias are given high points among special references. Confusion is common unless the differences are emphasized.

Having selected and found the reference source, the student is ready to make the first content note card, placing the sequence number from the tentative bibliography card that matches the reference in the upper right hand corner of a three-by-five-inch index card.

The content that has been identified as useful is noted on the card making certain that only a single idea is placed on a card. It does not matter that the card is not completely filled. The page(s) from which the information is extracted is to be included. If the content is reworded in the searcher's own words, giving page number(s) is sufficient. If the content is being quoted in exact words, the notes should be placed within quotation marks as well. If the single idea that is being recorded on the content card is too extensive for a single card, continue the information onto a second card. Note that the information is continued at the bottom of the first card and make sure that the codings appear on the second note card as well. Continuation cards might be clipped together.

The final step in writing a content note card is to place in the upper left hand corner of the card the attack outline number and letter which shows where this content fits into the attack outline plan. These cards should be filed according to the outline markings. There are two advantages to doing this. First, when the search is completed, the cards will be in order to write from with only minor rearrangement within each outline division. Second, keeping the cards in outline order allows the searcher to spot any areas that are omitted or too sparsely covered. Examples of content note cards:

II A   1
    Lee was born 1807, died 1870

                                          p. 3

III C 2   1
    Lee capitulated at Appomattox Court House on April 9, 1865, his forces having been pursued and completely surrounded by General Grant's forces.

                                         p. 54

When shortages of information are discovered, the student has several options. First, a reexamination of the materials used may provide the information if the omission was an oversight on the part of the notetaker. Second, additional sources may be found either in the same or another library. To find more sources, the student may need to ask for assistance from the library media center personnel. Third, if only a small quantity of the material is available, perhaps the outline needs to be reshaped a bit. Or finally, if no information can be found at all, the question, albeit a good and valid one, may need to be dropped from the outline and the paper entirely.

A summary of the procedures and systems to be used in preparing for and conducting the search is included on the following pages. The teacher might make this available to students as a quick reference during a search project.

Summary of Procedures and Systems for Organizing the Search Project

TIPS FOR SAVING TIME. 1. Use three-by-five-inch index cards (Slips of paper can be substituted but are more difficult to file and handle.) 2. Use the style sheet. 3. Be accurate. 4. Use coding whenever possible. 5. Use pen. Pencil smudges and is hard to read.

ATTACK OUTLINE. The attack outline does not include introduction, transitions, or conclusions. It is only an outline of the facts that must be acquired to construct the paper. When the paper is being written, the introductory remarks, the transitional sections, and the summary and concluding remarks *will* be incorporated. Since they grow out of the material that is collected, there is no need to try to fit them into the attack outline.

```
                              Outline
    I. ..........................................................
        A. .....................................................
        B. .....................................................
            1. .................................................
            2. .................................................
   II. ..........................................................
        A. .....................................................
            1. .................................................
            2. .................................................
            3. .................................................
        B. .....................................................
        C. .....................................................
```

TENTATIVE BIBLIOGRAPHY CARDS. Follow the sample card in the stylesheet. In addition, place sequential number in the order in which you find leads to the references in upper right hand corner of your cards. If you are working by types of references, indicate the type represented in the lower right hand corner.

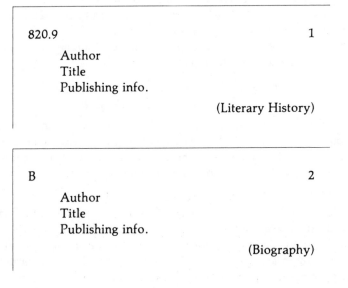

820.9   1

     Author
     Title
     Publishing info.

                   (Literary History)

B   2

     Author
     Title
     Publishing info.

                   (Biography)

```
Per.                                                3

    Author
    Title
    Publishing info.

                                         (Periodical)
```

CONTENT NOTE CARDS. Use coding to avoid rewriting information. The sequence number from the tentative bibliography cards is placed in the upper right hand corner; the appropriate attack outline section number is placed in the upper left hand corner.

Only *one* idea may be recorded on a note card. It does not matter that the card is not completely filled.

If exact words are being taken down, place them in quotation marks.

Be sure to note the pages used for each idea taken down.

```
I B 2                                               2
    ..........................................................
    ..........................................................
    ............
                                              p. 103
```

Information extracted by student, not a direct quote from the reference. No quotation marks needed. (Single idea only)

```
II C                                                1
      " ........................................................
    ..........................................................
    ............ "
                                              p. 56
```

Direct quotation from reference used. (Single idea only)

"
....
....
...."

p. 421

Another direct quotation. (Single idea only)

Writing the Search Paper

The time has come to prepare the first draft. The introductory remarks and the thesis statement are presented. Then the materials are worked through following the outline order. Each section needs to be linked with the previous one through a transitional statement or passage. Finally, the conclusion with its restatements and summarizations is used to tie the whole paper together and to prove or disprove the thesis statement.

The classroom teacher will find that the students usually need assistance in learning to develop a thesis statement. The value of such a statement in providing the coherent framework of a presentation (oral or written) is all too often overlooked by students. Indeed, unless the classroom teacher requires presentation of a thesis statement as part of the scoring and due date information, students tend to put off its development. Without the focus provided by a thesis statement right from the start, the student will waste much time.

A thesis, according to definition, is a proposition to be proved or maintained against argument. In a search paper, the thesis is a concise statement of the principal purpose of the paper, a single sentence which provides the focus for it. This proposition can be stated either positively or negatively, and the search paper should be constructed to support the statement. There are many sources of ideas to turn into thesis statements. For literary topics, literary criticism may be scanned for statements such as the following, taken from *Contemporary Literary Criticism*, volume fifteen, to provide examples of thesis statements.

The critic Rushworth M. Kidder has written that "There are distinct stylistic relationships between Cummings' paintings and his poetry, and an understand-

CARD CODING KEY

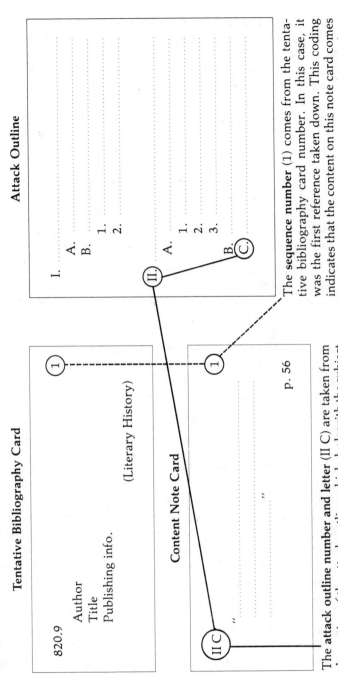

Tentative Bibliography Card

820.9

Author
Title
Publishing info.

(Literary History)

Attack Outline

I.
  A.
  B.
    1.
    2.

II.
  A.
    1.
    2.
    3.
  B.
  C.

Content Note Card

p. 56

The **sequence number** (1) comes from the tentative bibliography card number. In this case, it was the first reference taken down. This coding indicates that the content on this note card comes from the reference on that bibliography card.

The **attack outline number and letter** (II C) are taken from the section of the attack outline which deals with the subject of the content card. Note cards will be kept in outline order.

ing of them can help us to a sounder sense of his work."
The purpose of this paper will be to identify some of these
stylistic relationships.

According to critic Martha T. Halsey, "Buero Vallejo
often uses sets of opposing characters in his plays. The
egoist, usually the practical man of action, is contrasted
with the idealist or dreamer." In this paper, the plays
Almost a Fairy Tale and *The Dream Weaver* will be
examined to show that this contrast of characters is
evident.

Critic Martha T. Halsey has observed that "Buero
Vallejo believes that tragedy tries to show that catastrophe
is the consequence of man's errors, or his violations of
moral order. Buero's own plays underscore the element of
human responsibility...." In this paper, the plays...

Perhaps a social studies paper could be constructed around a
thesis statement such as, "President John F. Kennedy used his presidential powers effectively in bringing about a resolution of the
Cuban Missile Crisis." The information to be searched for would
need to identify the presidential powers, the actions taken by the
president, and evaluations of those actions. If the search showed
that the president's actions were ineffective rather than effective, the
student would only have to change his thesis statement from positive to negative and carry on from there.

Preparing Footnotes

The decision must be made—often by the classroom teacher—
whether footnotes will appear at the bottom of the pages of the paper
or in a separate section after the text of the paper and before the final
bibliography. When footnotes are placed at the bottom of the pages
they are numbered beginning with one on each page. However,
when they are placed in a notes section at the end of the paper, they
are numbered sequentially throughout the paper. In a long paper
broken into chapters, it may be desirable to list the notes by chapters.
In this case, each chapter begins with a number one note. Otherwise,
the triple digit note numbers become a nuisance.

One thing that slows up the conscientious classroom teacher
when grading search papers is making a reference check. Hours can
be spent in fruitless tracing of the material that has been plagiarized
by students. It is sensible, therefore, to design the search project in
such a way that plagiarism is held to a minimum, and, should any

verification of sources be necessary, it will be the student upon whom the burden falls and not the classroom teacher.

Too few classroom teachers insist that ideas be credited when they are not the student's own. Students may come to believe that if they change a word here or there they have met the requirements of honesty and original work, but this is not the case. If the student did not produce independently the idea used, then citation of the source is required. This is equally necessary whether the words were taken verbatim (in which case they should have been placed within quotation marks) or whether the idea is used and reworded slightly. Students, when faced with the expectation of complete integrity, complain that they will be unable to write down anything without crediting it, but the classroom teacher should take a firm stand. Obviously, information that is common knowledge need not be credited, but in the standard student paper, much that should be footnoted often is not.

When the classroom teacher is determined that students understand that they must properly recognize their sources, two actions become necessary. First, the classroom teacher must explain clearly the penalty of *a reduction of grade* that will result from a student's failure to credit sources accurately. Second, students must understand that the paper which contains passages that the teacher has reason to question will not be graded until the student has brought the references, as well as the notes used, to clarify the sources. The best way to accomplish this is to have included this information in the written assignment sheet at the very beginning of the project. In this way, the burden of proof is with the student, not the classroom teacher or the library media teacher. (see page 19.)

Students should be shown how to construct footnotes properly for both the direct and indirect use of ideas. The form of the footnote is the same. The only problem, really, is frequent student confusion about what should be recognized as being taken from someone else, and what should not.

Two short quotations from material written by Roger Tory Peterson in *Gardening with Wildlife* may be useful in illustrating the above points. In the first paragraph below, Peterson lists the rules he uses to identify the characteristics of wildlife. In the second paragraph, he discusses applying those rules to bird identification, but he also lists some special characteristics of common birds to encourage the novice bird watcher. Here are the two excerpts:

I have always preferred to concentrate on certain

easy-to-spot field marks rather than on the technical, taxonomic differences among wildlife's phyla and classes and orders. When dealing with an identification problem (such as: I know that's a mammal, but is it a woodchuck or a gopher?), I set aside scientific perspectives and run down this list of eight questions:

1. What's its size?
2. What's its shape in silhouette?
3. What's its dominant color?
4. Are there special field marks?
5. How does it behave?
6. How does it move?
7. What sound does it make?
8. Where does it live?

Then, with the answers, I turn to a field guide and can tell for sure that...it's a gopher! (page 25)

Don't let the wonderful variety of birds discourage you from getting acquainted with the comparatively small number of species which you will find nesting and feeding in your yard. Just remember my eight simple questions and repair to your field guides. However, I may be able to save you some seemingly impossible mix-ups in identifying similar birds if you will keep these identity clues in mind:
—The starling is the only black bird in your garden with a yellowish beak and a short tail. Don't confuse him with the grackle, which is a bit larger, has a dark beak, and a slightly longer tail, or with the cowbird, which has a brown head upon his black body.
—The house sparrow has a short, canary-like beak, and may often be observed "dust bathing" to clean off external parasites. It should not be confused with the house wren which is smaller and has a slender bill as well as a tail that often cocks up over its back. (page 31)

The student might write, based upon the excerpt, the following:

Roger Tory Peterson is a respected naturalist, well versed in the scientific process. However, he sometimes prefers to apply a less formal approach in order to identify a species and to rely upon the application of eight questions:

1. What's its size?
2. What's its shape in silhouette?
3. What's its dominant color?
4. Are there special field marks?
5. How does it behave?
6. How does it move?
7. What sound does it make?
8. Where does it live?[1]

Having answered these questions, he checks with a reliable field book to complete the identification.

Birds offer more difficult challenges because, although the same questions are helpful, there are a number of close look-alikes. Peterson helps the watcher by pointing out that a starling is the only black bird with a yellowish beak and short tail. The yellow beak clearly separates the starling from its look-alike, the grackle, which has a dark beak, or the cowbird which has a dark beak and also a brown head on its black body.[2]

The first footnote marks a direct quotation using the author's exact words. The borrowed words are placed within quotation marks or indented in block style (as in this case). The second footnote marks an indirect quotation. The ideas are borrowed although the exact words are not. In either case, footnotes are required, and their format will be identical. They would read:

[1]Roger Tory Peterson. "Your Guide to Garden Wildlife." *Gardening with Wildlife*. Washington, D.C.: National Wildlife Federation, 1974, p. 25.
[2]*Ibid.*, p. 31.

Because the two references are from the same source and follow each other, the shortcut *Ibid.* may be used.

Providing Illustrations and References to Illustrations

Classroom teachers have been known to suggest to students that the insertion of clippings or pictures would enhance a report or project paper. Most library media teachers vehemently disagree with such instructions. The classroom teacher may expect the students to use appropriate discarded material from home, but this is usually not what happens. Many students do not have home subscriptions to periodicals suitable for a topic they are using in their search project, and they are apt to use little imagination or initiative about where to obtain discards. The result, too often, is that materials in the library media center are clipped and ruined for other users.

Classroom teachers should join firmly with the library media teachers in mandating that students make photocopies (as permitted under the educational fair use doctrine of the most recent copyright law) of needed pages from a book or periodical if absolutely necessary to the sense of their presentation. It is far better, however, in most cases to describe the illustration and its impórtance to the paper and simply cite where it may be found in a book or magazine. There is seldom any necessity to paste pictures into a report. The important thing about pictures is what the student has gained from examining them. More students need to understand how to use illustrations effectively as sources of information without clipping them from the sources in which they were found.

In a student-written paper on advertising and the use of billboards, the following example demonstrates the use of an illustration as a reference:

> It is not true that there were only small signs used to advertise a business before the advent of large highway billboards. In fact, the walls of the business itself were often used as background for extensive advertising. An example of this can be seen in the picture of Longwell's Transfer, an early automobile rental agency located in El Paso, Texas, at the turn of the century. It would have been difficult to miss the fact that Longwell had hacks and automobiles for hire and for sale, and offered to claim baggage if baggage checks were left.[1]
>
> [1]Elna Bakker and Richard G. Lillard. The Great Southwest: The Story of a Land and Its People. Palo Alto, CA: American West Publishing Co., 1972, p. 264.

Another example of a student-written paper using nonprint materials as a reference source might resemble the following:

> The obvious pleasure the patients take from a visit made to the convalescent home by a Brownie Scout Troop is evident in their faces as shown in the filmstrip.[4]
>
> [4]Our Neglected Elders. Filmstrip. Social Issues Series. Holyoke, MI: Scope Education, 1974, frames 13-16.

Rewriting the Final Draft

When the student has finished the first draft of the paper this is a good time for the teacher and the student to go over the work before the final rewriting. Every paper needs to be refined and re-written from the first rough draft (quite possibly more than once) if the student's best work is to be finally evaluated and graded. This is the time for the classroom teacher to check for the possibility of phony references and page numbers. It is unfortunately true that in today's competitive climate a few students will try to get away with dishonest shortcuts. It is especially true that with a teacher new to a school, there will be a certain amount of testing by students of teacher savvy and alertness. One rather common ploy is to acquire someone's else's project paper (a previously successful one, of course) and retype a cover page and bibliography—these being the pages that teachers tend to write comments on. Some teachers do not do a thorough correction job when they read the paper for grading and there are many papers to mark at once so pages are unmarred by teacher corrections, making cheating easier. Sometimes, under pressure of time, a classroom teacher will only glance at the body of the paper and examine the bibliography for currency. Type faces that do not match should always be noted.

Most such student gambits can be "response blocked" by an alert team of the classroom teacher and the library media teacher which has planned ahead. In order to assure that the student gains the experience that the project is intended to provide, to help the student produce effectively and with integrity, and to assist the classroom teacher in controlling the progress and grading of search papers, the methods described herein do help significantly.

Preparing the Final Bibliography

Now the search paper should be nearly completed. All that remains is that a cover sheet has to be prepared and the final bibliography has to be organized and typed. Up to this point, the tentative bibliography cards will have been kept in sequential order, making the final sorting easier. Cards for references that proved useless or that could not be obtained should now be discarded. The remaining cards, which match the footnotes, should be arranged in alphabetical order, using the author's last name when the material is signed or the title of the reference when the material is unsigned (as is the case with many reference tools). Once all the references are typed in alphabetical order following the prescribed style, the final bibliography and the project are completed.

7. Search Projects and Activities

The library media teacher gets as much satisfaction from a search project that goes well as do the students and the classroom teacher; and having the library media teacher as part of the team lends interest and scope to the undertaking. For the involved library media teacher, providing ideas for units and helping to shape them into usable projects becomes an important part of daily activity. Students benefit from the sharing of success and good relationships between classroom and library media teachers. It is all but inevitable that teachers who have an opportunity to demonstrate their own creativity through interaction with the library media center and its professional staff, become much more effective teachers—and know this.

I have had the pleasure of working with a number of excellent classroom teachers who have initiated interesting and highly effective approaches to the search paper project for their classes. In one instance, a social studies teacher produced topics in this subject which called for the use of a broad cross section of materials and also challenged the students to use their own imaginative thought while learning about Medieval and Renaissance periods in history, with the result that the possibility of boredom vanished.

In another instance, the classroom teacher waited until the start of the second semester to do the search paper project. During the first semester he studied his students carefully and began to put ideas together for individual topics. He was successful not only because he had studied his students but also because he was enough of a scholar himself to be able to draw from literature in a way that made possible his goal of complete individualization. For example, a student who was well versed in musical composition was given the opportunity to write about DeQuincy's use of a formula for creative writing and to make a comparison between the two forms of creating within the boundaries of a firm set of rules. Another student who did not take well to criticism found himself hunting for Byron's reaction to having had his works panned by the *Edinburgh Review* critic. This may be nearly the ultimate in matching subject with student, but it suggests a direction toward which any classroom teacher could strive and achieve in some degree at least. The latter assignment mentioned not only caught the interest of the student but was an excellent exercise in using primary sources.

Admittedly, this type of individualized approach calls for some teacher effort. The classroom teacher can begin to keep a card file of ideas for topics and assignments, adding a card whenever a new idea presents itself. There will soon be enough ideas collected so that a totally individualized assignment can be made and a really stimulating search begun. The students themselves can be a good source of suggestions for interesting topics, and these can be added to the file for future reference.

When a topic file is well stocked with idea cards, different combinations of these can be assembled to shape the thrust and content of student papers and reports easily and quickly. The effort made to supply students with assigned topics or a choice of topics from which to select not only helps to assure a higher level of content to be produced, read, and graded; it also reduces the ease with which one year's papers can be picked up and "adapted" by the next year's students. But despite all the exciting possibilities, there are still all too many teachers throughout the country who either assign the same tired topics year after year to succeeding groups or who, at the other extreme, send students off on search projects virtually without guidance or preparation.

The references and techniques learned by the classroom teacher with one classroom group become a permanent instructional tool for that teacher, ready for use with another group of students, but the topic possibilities are almost endless. The small amount of time required for annual upgrading and refurbishing of good techniques with the addition of new topic ideas is minimal, especially after the habit is formed and the coalition of classroom teacher and library media teacher is in good operating order. The increase of student interest and in student growth in independent learning, coupled with the increased satisfaction of the teaching team, make it all worthwhile.

What follows are some sample unit and assignment sheets that have been worked out, some of them by classroom teachers alone, some by classroom teachers in collaboration with the library media teacher, and others by the library media teacher alone.

Acknowledgment and thanks is made to the following classroom and subject teachers, from Ridgefield High School in Connecticut, whose work is included in the collection of samples that follows: Elizabeth Arneth, Valentine Ashe, Steven Blumenthal, Jacqueline Bouton, Nancy Bradley, Nancy Dignon, Vallerie Foerster, and John Sullivan—all of the English Department; Rachael Black-Ungar, John Suttich, and Margaret Vallerie, Social Studies Department; Regina Finney, Mathematics Department; Shirley Rauson, Chemistry Department; and John Tekian, Art Department. Working with all of them has been a pleasant combination of challenge and joy.

Diagnostic Testing

Reference is made in chapter four to the use of paper and pencil diagnostic quizzes. A number of basic skills are included in the following diagnostic sheets. The user is reminded that diagnostic testing, important as it is, is no substitute for practical application.

The H, P, and R listed at the end of these sheets means High, Pass, or Remediation Needed. Often merely going over a sheet of this sort in class is enough to refresh the student's mind. If, however, there is an area of great weakness, the remediation work is called for. When added work is needed to upgrade a skill, tapes and worksheets, transparencies, filmstrips, and other informational material that can be used independently are placed on reserve. The student is required to view and/or listen, take notes, or answer specific questions in areas of weakness.

CATALOG CARD

Answer the questions below the sample card basing your answers on the card.

Ref.   POLITICAL SCIENCE—BIBLIOGRAPHY
016.32   Harmon, Robert Bartlett, 1932–
         Literature of political science; a biblio-
         graphic guide / by Robert Bartlett
         Harmon. — New York : Scarecrow Press,
         1965.
             388 p. ; 22 cm.
         A guide to the literature of political sci-
         ence including fiction and biography from
         1850 to the present.

Author_____ Copyright_____
Subject _____
Title _____
Subtitle _____
Short title_____
Are there pictures?_____ Number of pages_____
Size of book_____ Publisher_____
What is a bibliography?_____
Would a book written in 1966 be included?_____
Would the book be a help for the period of the War of 1812?_____
What is an annotation?_____
What does one do with an annotation?_____

What is the book's call number?_____
        H_____
        P _____
        R _____

UNABRIDGED DICTIONARY

**Read the following example taken from an unabridged dictionary
and use it to answer the questions that follow the example.**

em blem (em'blĕm; -blẹm; -blĭm), n. [L. *emblema, -atis,*
inlaid work, that which is put on, fr. Gr. *emblema,* fr.
emballein to throw, lay, put in, fr. *en* in + *ballein* to
throw.]
1. Inlaid or mosaic work. *Obs.* 2. A picture accompanied
with a motto. 3. A visible sign of an idea. 4. A symbolic
object used as a heraldic device or badge. SYN.—Device,
badge, figure, image.

How many syllables does the word have_____
How many pronunciations are given for the word? _____
If the word came at the end of a line of typing, where could it be
divided? _____
What information is given within brackets? _____
What does SYN. stand for?_____
What does *Obs.* indicate?_____
What part of speech is the word?_____ How do you know?__
What is the difference between an abridged and an unabridged
dictionary? _____

_____
_____

H_____
P _____
R _____

Diagnostic Library Skills Test   Name_____

INDEXES   Date _____

An example is given below for each of several types of indexes. Each example is followed by a series of questions. Answer each set of questions basing your answers on the example which precedes them.

1. Reader's Guide

BURGER, Warren Earl

> Chief justice looks at crime and the courts, interview, por Read Digest 98:113 + Ap '71
> Words for a contentious profession; excerpts from address. Time 97:52 My 31 '71

> about

> Plea for civility. por Time 97:52 My 31 '71
> Chief justice Burger, R. A. Davies. Atlan M. 85:114–20 My '71

Subject _____
In what magazines will one find information about the subject?_____
In what magazines will one find information by the subject?_____
Where can one find a picture of the subject?_____
Where does one find explanations of abbreviations used?_____
When asking for a magazine from the school library stacks, what information must be provided by the student?_____
Explain in detail everything in the entry *following* the name of the magazine in the *first* reference given in the example._____

_____

_____

2. *New York Times Index* *

> JURIES and Jury Duty. See also Courts—Calif, My 2, 3, 5, 8. Subjects of cases.

> Ed urges passage of pending NYS legis to permit judges to question prospective jurors, My 1, 32:2

> U.S. Sup Ct, 6–3, upholds const of states granting juries the right 'to pronounce life or death in capital cases' and of common practice by which juries decide guilt and

---

*The *New York Times* is available on microfilm about six weeks after the paper is published.

immediately determine whether death penalty will be imposed, without hearing further evidence, McGautha-Crampton cases, My 4, 1:8; ed criticizes Sup Ct decision on capital punishment, calls for clear standards to guide juries deliberations in such cases, My 6, 42:2

What is the subject?_____
Where does one find additional or related information?_____

Copy the information needed to locate editorial opinion on the subject._____
Copy information needed to locate news reporting on the subject._

Explain in detail the entry copied to locate news reporting. Include all letters and numbers._____

3. Cumulative Indexes

Explain what is meant by a cumulative index, give an example of one, and tell why it is important to the student to be aware of cumulative indexes._____

4. Books Index

Churchill, Sir Winston, 56, 79 ff, 143.
Clifford, Clark, 40, 119, 155-163, 246 n.

Which reference for each entry will have the largest amount of information on the subject?_____
How do you know?_____

5. Encyclopedia Index

MELANESIA, isls., Pac. D. 15-121; 4-109a; 12-134B; 9-315d.

Which entry will have the largest amount of information on the subject?_____
How do you know?_____
Three of the references include letters as well as numbers. Explain each part of these three entries._____

H_____
P _____
R _____

Name_____

Date _____

ATLASES

Atlases may be historical, modern, or deal with a special subject, but in any instance one should start to use an atlas through its_____.
A map of smaller size may cover a larger geographic area than another map because of_____.
Central city maps are frequently found where in atlases?_____
_____

A gazetteer differs from an atlas in that the gazetteer_____
_____ .

If a map reference read Atlanta, Ga., 451,500. . . . C2 p83 what would each of the following mean?

        451,500 _____

           C2 _____

          p83 _____

Normally, the top of a map is what direction?_____
A topographical map indicates_____

H_____
P _____
R _____

Diagnostic Library Skills Test

OUTLINING

Use the following form to outline each group of topics below.
Answer on a separate sheet of lined paper.

Title (all-inclusive term)
I. (Roman numeral)
   A. (upper case letter)
      1. (Arabic numeral)
         a. (lower case letter)

1.

Time
Calendars
Clocks
Days of week
Months
Roman calendar
Egyptian calendar
Water clock
Mayan calendar
Hebrew calendar
Sundials
Pendulum clock
Daylight saving
Weight clock
Electric clock
Time zones
International date line

3.

Dogs
Training
Exercising
Oral commands
Housing
Leash commands
Feeding
Whistle commands

2.

Foods
Peas
Apples
Peaches
Fruits
Tomatoes
Potatoes
Onions
Strawberries
Vegetables
Celery
Carrots
Bananas

4.

Sports and games
Baseball
Basketball
Badminton
Racquet games
Water polo
Tennis
Water sports
Field games
Swimming
Soccer
Scuba diving
Softball
Racquet ball

	5.	6.
	Stamp collecting	Countries
	Airplane models	Elephants
	Hobbies	Egypt
	Buying stamps	Nigeria
	Building models	Giraffe
	Automobile models	Ghana
	Gardening	Driver ant
	Trading stamps	Animals
	Train models	Africa
	Planting seeds	Rivers
	Mounting stamps	Antelope
	Rocket models	Nile River
	Using fertilizer	Tsetse fly
	Weeding	Congo River
	Watering	Insects

H_____
P _____
R _____

Alphabetizing

Students exposed initially to alphabetizing in elementary schools are taught letter-by-letter alphabetizing. This is because that is the system traditionally used in dictionaries, and at the time the students are learning to use language dictionaries.

When are they taught that there is a second way of using the alphabet to arrange materials alphabetically? This does not always happen. Students who do not understand the word-by-word system of alphabetizing are handicapped in a search project.

The card catalog is traditionally alphabetized by the word-by-word system, and this causes students to miss material that is there for their use. Reference books are arranged by either system depending upon the indexer's preference. Students are usually amazed to find that encyclopedias vary in the system used. There is no need for students to try to memorize which reference uses which system, but they should become familiar with both systems and develop the habit of making sure that they are using the proper system.

Exercises such as those that follow will prove useful in emphasizing this skill.

Two Ways To Alphabetize
Worksheet

Name_____

Date _____

Read the following lesson on alphabetizing carefully to learn about the two systems used. Then complete the exercises which follow.

There are two alphabetic arrangement systems each using the same twenty-six letters, *A* through *Z*. One is called letter-by-letter, the other word-by-word. The letter-by-letter system is used in dictionaries. It is the system you learned in elementary school. Simply strike off identical letters until you come to something different and compare those letters. The word-by-word system is used in card catalogs. In this system you use only the first word for alphabetizing purposes. Stop at the end of that first word. When several alphabetized first words are the same, then look at the second words.

The problem arises when you use reference books. The editor decides which system to use. Some encyclopedias use the letter-by-letter system; some use the word-by-word system. Handbooks may also use either system.

You must make sure you are using the same system the editor is using. A good test is to look up these words: new, old, north, south. If the words appear consecutively and are not interfiled with other words, the word-by-word system is being used. In a large encyclopedia index or card catalog, the entries you want could be inches (if not whole pages or drawers) apart depending upon the alphabetic system being used. So, be careful! Don't cheat yourself!

1. There are _____ ways to alphabetize.
2. Word-by-word alphabetizing is always used in _____
   _____.
3. Letter-by-letter alphabetizing is always used in_____.
4. Both systems are used in _____ _____. It is the editor of the book who decides which system to use.
5. In letter-by-letter alphabetizing, all letters in the string of words are
   _____ _____ into a single word. In word-by-word alphabetizing, only the letters in the _____ word are considered. When first words are the same, then the letters in the _____ word are considered.
6. In the two columns of alphabetized words below, column one is done by the _____ method and column two is done by the _____ method.

New Bedford	Newark Times
New Hampshire	New Bedford
New Jersey	Newberg, John
New Port Terrace	New Hampshire
New York	New Jersey
New Zealand	Newport News
Newark Times	New Port Terrace
Newberg, John	Newton, John
Newport News	New York
Newton, Isaac	New Zealand

7. Number the list of words below in alphabetical order following both methods.

Letter-by-letter		Word-by-word
2	SOUTH AMERICA	1
3	SOUTH BEND	2
4	SOUTH CAROLINA	3
5	SOUTH DAKOTA	4
8	SOUTH SHORE	5
10	SOUTH ZEALAND	6
1	SOUTHABY	7
6	SOUTHEAST	8
7	SOUTHINGTON	9
9	SOUTHWORTH	10

8. What system of alphabetizing is used in each of the following reference books? Find the book, look at its arrangement, and decide which system is used by the editor. Words in the index such as *big, little, new,* or *old* give you easy places to check the system if you are uncertain. You ought to be able to tell by looking at any page you open to.

Americana Encyclopedia	_____
Benet's Reader's Encyclopedia	_____
Oxford Companion to Music	_____
Dictionary of American History	_____
Who's Who	_____
Encyclopaedia Britannica	_____
Collier's Encyclopedia	_____

Encyclopedias

Name_____

Date _____

TOPIC:___*Shopping Cente_*___*___

1. Indicate which alphabetic system is used for each of the encyclopedias listed and indicate how much coverage is given your topic in each.

	System Used	*Pagings*
Americana	_____	_____
Collier's	_____	_____
International	_____	_____
Compton's	_____	_____
World Book	_____	_____
Britannica (old)	_____	_____

2. Compare coverage in each section of *Britannica* (new) listed below.

Propedia—_____

Micropedia—_____

Macropedia— _____

3. List only the alphabetic system used in each of these literary handbooks.

Penguin_____

Benet's *Reader's Encyclopedia*_____

Oxford Companions (any)_____

New Century Handbook of English Literature_____

Thrall _____

---

*Each student should have a different topic.

Bibliographic Abbreviations

Attention rarely seems to be given to the use of abbreviations. Students need to learn that esoteric abbreviations will be explained traditionally in the front of a reference book. This is a responsibility of the author or editor.

On the other hand, there are many standard bibliographic abbreviations that are rarely explained in the front of reference books. It is expected that the student who has advanced to the level at which the book is to be used will somehow have mastered the use of these abbreviations. It just does not happen this way! Attention should be called to the use and meaning of abbreviations.

One of the best lists of standard bibliographic abbreviations may be found in *The New Library Key* by Margaret G. Cook (3rd ed., New York: H.W. Wilson, 1975.). She has omitted [*sic*], but otherwise the list is reasonably inclusive. Once students understand these abbreviations and the information that is acquired through their use, they seem to be surprised at how frequently they are encountered. Because they have been in the habit of skipping over the unknown abbreviations, they have not realized what they were missing.

ABBREVIATIONS
IDENTIFICATION

Abbreviations which are unusual or specialized will be explained by
the author in the beginning of the reference book in which they are
used. However, there are a number of standard abbreviations which
are not usually explained. These the student is expected to know on
sight. Explain each of the following by telling in English what the
abbreviation means, or what the reader is expected to do when he
finds it in the text.

abr._____	infra_____
anon._____	supra_____
bibl. (or bibliog.)_____	loc. cit._____
c. 1290 (NOT copyright)_____	n.d. _____
cf. _____	o.p. _____
ed._____	pam. _____
e.g. _____	passim_____
enl. _____	pl. (NOT plural)_____
ff. _____	pseud. _____
fl. (or flor.)_____	q.v. _____
ibid._____	rev. _____
i.e._____	trans. (or tr.)_____
illus. _____	[sic] _____
front._____	v. or vol._____

H_____
P _____
R _____

Abbreviation Application Name _____
Worksheet Date _____

Explain each of the abbreviations in the sample bibliographic entries
given below. Be sure to give complete explanations. An answer sheet
follows the samples.

SAMPLE BIBLIOGRAPHIC ENTRIES
1. Hafiz. Pseud. of Shams-ud-din Muhammad (c1300–1388).
   Persian poet.
2. Leonardo da Vinci. . . The best known are *The Adoration of
   the Magi* in the Uffizi; *The Madonna in the Grotto* (c1495)
   and the *Mona Lisa* (1503) both in the Louvre.
3. SHAKESPEARE, WM.
   18   If it will feed nothing else, it will
        feed my revenge.
        Merchant of Venice Act III, Sc., 1, L. 55.
   19   Now, infidel, I have you on the hip.
        Ibid. Act IV, Sc., 1, L. 334.
4. BROADHEAD'S ALLEGHENY CAMPAIGN (1779). Col.
   Daniel Broadhead set out from Fort Pitt,[qv] August 11, 1779,
   with 600 regulars, volunteers, and a few Delaware[qv]
   warriors against the Senaca[qv] on the upper Allegheny.
5. [1]Smith, John. *Ways of Talk*, (N.Y.: Houghton, 1964) p. 14.
   [2]Hart, Matt. *Communication*, (N.Y.: Harper, n.d.) p. 614.
   [3]*Ibid*.
   [4]Smith. *loc. cit.*
   [5]Smith. *op. cit.*, Ch. 3, *passim*.
6. Cezanne, Paul, 184, 192–194, 216 ff., 297,
        302, 206
        autobiography, 266
        technique, 267
7. Equipment, 190; arrangement of,
        292, 306–10, 425–26; bibliog.
        316–17; book trucks, 301–303;
        homemade equipment, 295 sqq.,
        pl. 306; newspaper racks, 40.
8. 811 Arbuthnot, May Hill, 1884– comp.
        Time for poetry. Illus. by Rainey Bennett.
        Rev. ed. Chicago. Scott, Foresman. 1959.
        512 p. bibl. 22 cm.

"A teacher's anthology of children's poetry."
9. 932 Bollingen Foundation
The tomb of Ramesses VI. New York. Pantheon
Books. 1954. o.p.

2 v. front. illus. 32 cm.
10. Listed are the facts of publication, i.e., place of publication, name of publisher and date (copyright date of edition used).
11. A number of painters have used this technique; e.g., Rembrandt and Halls.
12. The Alhambra (supra) exemplifies Moorish styling.
13. Tombstone, Arizona (fl. 1840's) has become a ghost town.
14. I wish I were single again.
I Married a Wife (19th Cen.) Anon.
15. Frost develops the theme using New England settings; cf. Gates' *Desert Song.*

ANSWER SHEET
1. *Pseud.*_____
   c. _____
2. *c.* (What is the difference between *c* in 1 and in 2?)_____
3. *Ibid.* _____
4. qv. (all of them) _____
   _____
   _____
5. n.d. _____
   Ibid. _____
   loc. cit. _____
   op. cit. _____
   passim. _____
6. ff._____
7. bibliog. _____
   sqq. _____
   pl._____
8. comp. _____
   Illus. _____
   Rev. _____
   ed. _____
   bibl. _____
   cm. _____
9. o.p. _____
   v. _____

front. _____

illus. _____

cm. _____

10. i.e. _____

11. e.g. _____

12. supra. _____

13. fl. _____

14. Anon. _____

15. cf. _____

Subject Terminology in Indexes

A major problem for the inexperienced searcher is to learn to think in the terms used by the indexer. A project that can be useful either as a search for topics and sources only or, in an enlarged version, to include the actual writing of a short paper is one based on the *Reader's Guide to Periodical Literature* and the *New York Times Index* (or any other available newspaper index). The point being made is that the same content is listed differently in various indexes. It all depends upon the indexer's terminology.

A structured worksheet is helpful with this project. All dates have been made retrospective for the reason that when students are allowed to use current periodicals, they usually do not use the index. Instead, they simply pick up a current issue and work from it. This lesson is meant to give practice in using the indexes to find specific content. Without the use of required dates, much of the value of the lesson may be lost. Dates used in the worksheet must match the holdings of the library media center being used.

It is possible to enlarge the project by asking the student to trace terminology used to identify the topic over one or more decades. The student may be able to find the date when the topic was introduced in the indexes. Again, assignment requirements are subject to the indexing and periodical and newspaper holdings available.

Index Terminology
Worksheet

Name_____

Date _____

Assigned letter_____

Using your assigned letter

1. Choose a topic for a short paper and write, in your own terms, the content descriptor. (Examples: Cloud formations, house plant bugs, western canyons).

   Topic chosen _____

2. Look up your topic content in the two indexes listed below and fill information in the blanks as you find it. Note that the topic content may appear in different terminology in different indexes, and it may be different within each index depending upon the year of the index.

   New York Times Index
   Year used_____ Pages in index where found_____
   Terminology of subject heading used_____
   Location of article in newspaper: Month_____
   Page_____ Column_____ Section (if given)_____
   If your teacher instructs you to, using the newspaper itself, also provide the title and author of the article, which are not given in the index.
   Title of article_____
   Author of article_____

   Reader's Guide to Periodical Literature
   Year used_____ Pages in index where found_____
   Terminology of subject heading used_____
   Location of article in magazine:_____
   Name of magazine_____ Month_____ Day_____
   Volume number_____ Pages_____
   Title of article_____
   Author of article_____

3. Trace the use of terminology in the index by checking the index volumes to determine the earliest date the heading you used for the "Reader's Guide" was used in the index.

   Date_____

Was a different term used for this topic content in earlier years?___

_____

If yes, why do you suppose the changes in terminology took place?
_____

If no, does this date mark the invention, discovery, or beginning of the topic?_____

_____

4. If your teacher instructs you to do so, read the newspaper and periodical articles found in both indexes and write a short paper based on them.

Use of Retrospective   Name_____
Materials Worksheet   Date _____

Choose a topic for a short paper and write it in the space provided. Using "Reader's Guide to Periodical Literature", select articles that fall within the dates given. Fill in the blanks as the information is found. If your teacher asks you to, write the paper.

Topic ___*Bus driver*___ *

Use indexing from 1960 to 1965:
Name of index used _____ Date of index_____
Terminology of subject heading used_____
Pages of index_____
Name of magazine_____ Year_____
Month_____ Volume_____ Page(s)_____
Title of article_____
Author of article_____

Use indexing from 1965 to 1970:
Name of index used _____ Date of index_____
Terminology of subject heading used_____
Pages of index_____
Name of magazine_____ Year_____
Month_____ Volume_____ Page(s)_____
Title of article_____
Author of article_____

Use indexing from 1970 to 1975:
Name of index used _____ Date of index_____
Terminology of subject heading used_____
Pages of index_____
Name of magazine_____ Year_____
Month_____ Volume_____ Page(s)_____
Title of article_____
Author of article_____

_____

*There is a shortage of indexed articles on the topic per se in the years 1970–1975, so this is an example of how to do a related substitution. There is no cross reference from our topic *bus drivers* to *motor bus drivers* in most of the indexes. However, by using a cross reference from *bus* to *motor bus* one finds all the other related *bus* topics—including some relating to *bus drivers*.

Dictionaries

Review the coverage, arrangement, and use of the unabridged dictionary. Give attention to the differences between an abridged and an unabridged dictionary: scope, format, special features, suitability for age level, and purpose. Discuss specialized dictionaries. Students need to know that they exist for every field and are a beginning point in many searches. Fact sheets are included for both language and specialized dictionaries. These may be used as teacher references or distributed to students.

Provide each student with a card upon which is written the call number and the title of a specialized dictionary. A list of specialized dictionaries is included for your reference. Either assign the cards to students or allow them to be drawn by chance. Ask the student to find the book, examine it in terms of the characteristics and purposes discussed in class, and then write a sales pitch to interest classmates in owning the specialized dictionary.

When the project is completed, students can share their writings in class. They usually are amazed at how many different specialized dictionaries there are and how helpful these books can be. The project combines a writing assignment with a reference skills experience.

Language Dictionaries Fact Sheet

1. We think of language dictionaries first because we use them the most.
2. Language dictionaries are either *abridged* (shortened) or unabridged. Unabridged dictionaries contain more words (ranging from 250,000 to 600,000 +), but they do not include all the words in the language.
3. There are over one million words in English.
4. Unabridged dictionaries contain the most frequently used words in the language.
5. Unabridged dictionaries may contain several special sections such as gazetteers (geographic data), biographical sections, historical date lists, history of the language, and guides for using the dictionary.
6. Unabridged dictionaries may also be *encyclopedic*, meaning that the content of these special sections is distributed throughout the main text.
7. A typical word entry includes pronunciation, syllabication, part of speech, derivation, and meanings. Dictionaries report words that are in use rather than the words that "should" be used. Only Samuel Johnson created a dictionary that claimed to be an arbiter of correctness. Some dictionaries list oldest meanings first. Sometimes these meanings are marked *Obs.*, meaning obsolete (*Webster's New International, second edition*). Some dictionaries list slang and informal meanings in the main section (*Webster's New International, third edition*, 1961). Some dictionaries list the newest meanings first (*Funk & Wagnall's New Standard*).
8. Some dictionaries are British English and have different meanings, spellings, and pronunciations than American English. Be aware of this when you use *Chambers Twentieth Century Dictionary* or the *Oxford Dictionary of the English Language.*.
9. British English dictionaries are especially good for word derivations. Derivation means the tracing of the historical movement of the word. A word may have started in Greek or Latin and moved into French before appearing in English or it may have started in English and moved into some other language.

Specialized Dictionaries Fact Sheet

1. All subjects have dictionaries and encyclopedias. (See the partial list following the assignment below.)
2. Sometimes dictionaries are called glossaries or handbooks.
3. All contain short, simple entries that serve to identify the topic. (The encyclopedia expands on the topic, and the specialized encyclopedia goes into depth and great detail.)
4. Points to consider when judging a specialized dictionary:
   a. Read the subtitle. This gives you hints for limitations the editor has intended to use. Do not fault the editor for leaving out material that has been left out intentionally.
   b. Read the introduction or preface. This tells you the author or editor's intent, as well as the purpose of the book.
   c. Are the proper words included for your use? Are there only the basic (easy) ones or many detailed terms meant for the specialist in the field?
   d. Are the definitions given in simple, direct language, or do you need another dictionary to interpret the words used in the definitions?
   e. Consider the format. Is there a good layout with easy to read print? Is it pleasing to the eye with enough open space?
   f. Is the author an authority in the field or just someone interested in publishing?
   g. Is this information easily available elsewhere or does this book fill a unique need?

ASSIGNMENT: Locate the specialized dictionary assigned to you in the library media center. Examine it in light of the seven points given above. Then write a sales pitch for the students in your class explaining to them why they would be wise to purchase this particular specialized dictionary.

TITLES OF SPECIALIZED DICTIONARIES

Religion
Dictionary of Biblical Allusions in English Literature
Dictionary of Buddhism
Dictionary of Saints
Interpreter's Dictionary of the Bible

Social Sciences
Black's Law Dictionary

Crescent Dictionary of American Politics
Dictionary of American Government and Politics
Dictionary of Black Culture
Dictionary of Business and Economics
Dictionary of Costume
Dictionary of the History of Ideas
Dictionary of Modern Economics
Dictionary of Mythology, Folklore & Symbols
Dictionary of Modern Revolution
Dictionary of Psychology
Dictionary of Stock Market Terms
News Dictionary

Language

Dictionary of Americanisms
Dictionary of Cliches
Dictionary of Catch Phrases
Dictionary of Contemporary American Usage
Dictionary of Early English
Dictionary of English Word Roots
Dictionary of American Homophones and Homographs
Dictionary of Modern English Usage
Dictionary of Slang and Unconventional English
Dictionary of Spanish Idioms
Dictionary of Symbols
Dictionary of Word and Phrase Origins
Eponyms Dictionaries Index

Science

Dictionary of Ecology
Dictionary of Mathematics
Dictionary of Scientific Terms
Dictionary of Sharks
Dinosaur Dictionary
McGraw Hill Dictionary of Scientific and Technical Terms

Fine Arts

Dictionary of American Portraits
Dictionary of the Decorative Arts
Dictionary of Italian Painting
Dictionary of Marks: Pottery & Porcelain
Dictionary of Painting
Dictionary of Modern Painting

Harvard Dictionary of Music
Dictionary of Contemporary Music
Grove's Dictionary of Music and Musicians
Dictionary of Stamps in Color

Literature

Dictionary of Fictional Characters
Dictionary of Literary Pseudonyms
Dictionary of Literary Terms
Dictionary of Phrase & Fable
Dictionary of Quotations
Dictionary of World Literature

History

Dictionary of Chivalry
Dictionary of Modern History, 1789–1945
Dictionary of American History
Dictionary of American Biography
Dictionary of Scientific Biography
Dictionary of National Biography
Webster's Biographical Dictionary
Baker's Biographical Dictionary of Musicians

Miscellaneous

Dictionary of Drugs
Dictionary of International Food and Cooking Terms
Dictionary of Technical Terms
Trade Names Dictionary

Biographical Searches

After instruction has been provided so that the students are aware that basic biographical references are arranged according to whether the person is living or long deceased, where the person lived, or what the person did, the use of a worksheet provides practice. Three such worksheets are included. Teacher instructions for each follow.

Commonality

Select the names of three persons, the first one current, the second from some years back, and the third one older still, who have something in common. Provide the students with the names (and possibly the dates of their lives) and ask them to discover and prove the commonality. Some students who recognize one or two of the trio may jump to the correct conclusion without ever having used the references unless they must provide proof. Therefore, call numbers, authors and titles of sources, as well as volume and page numbers should be required. Examples for this exercise are given below. Each group of three names is followed by the commonality among those people. These or other similar groups of names may be filled in on the worksheet for assignment to students.

Mick Jagger, O. Henry, and Sisyphus. *The rolling stone*

Theodor Seuss Geisel, Elizabeth Meriwether Gilmer, and Marie Henry Beyle. *All used pseudonyms: Dr. Seuss, Dorothy Dix, and Stendhal.*

Leo Africanus (also known as Johannes Leo and al-Hasan ibn-Muhammod a-Wazzan), Henry Morton Stanley, and Joy Adamson. *All wrote about Africa and their adventures there.*

Victor Borge, Jacob Riis, and Jonas Bronck. *All born in Denmark, and all have made contributions to adopted country, the United States. (Bronck's name gave rise to the area of New York City called the Bronx.)*

Cher Bono, Maria Tallchief, and Knud Rasmussen. *Born of mixed ancestry*

Henry Moore, Emil Frey, and John F. Blondel. *Holes in their work: sculptor, Swiss cheese manufacturer, inventor of doughnut machine*

Maurzico Pollini, Nicolo Paganini, and Arcangelo Corelli. *All Italian musicians—pianist and two violinists.*

John Crowe Ransom, Sydney Dobell, and Oliver Goldsmith. *Poets who died 100 years apart: 1974, 1874, 1774*

Ada Louise Huxtable, Pierre L'Enfant, and John Nash (1752–1835). *All city planners*

John W. Warner, Prince Philip, and Robert Browning. *Wives named Elizabeth*

Jean-Pierre Rampal, King Frederick of Prussia, and Jean-Baptiste Loeillet. *All flute players*

Julia Child, Juliet Corson, and Martha Distell. *All involved in cooking schools: Corson ran the first cooking school in the U.S.; Distell founded the famous Cordon Bleu.*

Herbert Lawrence Block, Thomas Nast, and Martin Disteli. *Cartoonists.*

Commonality Worksheet

Name_____

Date _____

There is a commonality among the three people named below. Find and prove it.

Commonality_____

1. _____

References used: _____ Pages_____

Details: _____

2. _____

References used: _____ Pages_____

Details: _____

3. _____

References used: _____ Pages_____

Details: _____

Who's Who

Students select a family name identical or similar to their own. An entry two inches long is found for this name and rewritten into good English. Abbreviations should be translated and the sequence of information changed. The reason for having students rewrite the material provided into a readable biographical tract is that students often translate abbreviations out of context. They may also fail to "read" the punctuation in the biographical entry and not get accurate information. The reason for having the student rearrange the order in which the information is given in the reference book is that this also is a skill to be learned. The information appears in a formula sequence. Changing its order and applying some creativity in use of information is a higher level skill. It may be that for less able students the requirement would be only to translate the abbreviations.

Who's Who Worksheet   Name_____

Date _____

Choose a name that is the same or similar to your family name. Select an entry in a Who's Who reference that is two inches long. Translate every abbreviation, and then rewrite the information in your own words with the order changed so that it becomes a readable biographical tract. Under no circumstances should you follow the sequence of information given in the reference.

Name chosen:_____

Reference used:_____

_____

_____

_____

_____

_____

_____

Nicknames

Select nicknames of famous people and ask students to give their real names, using a reference book such as *American Nicknames*. A list and an exercise using nicknames of American presidents follow.

Nicknames Worksheet

Name_____

Date _____

Using the reference book American Nicknames, identify the president whose nickname is given and explain why or how he got it.

President's nickname_____

President's name_____

Answer found on page_____

Explanation of how or why the nickname was given the president:

_____
_____
_____
_____
_____
_____
_____
_____
_____
_____
_____
_____
_____

PRESIDENTIAL NICKNAMES

Stocking Foot Orator	Old Tippecanoe
Idol of Ohio	Accidental President
Little Ben	Old Rough and Ready
Chinese Harrison	Young Hickory
Dumb Prophet	First Dark Horse
Buffalo Hangman	Duel Fighter
Old Veto	Hero of New Orleans
Dude President	Last Cocked Hat
Prince Arthur	Era of Good Feeling President

Bull Moose
Trust Buster
Four Eyes
Mr. Republican
Phrasemaker
Schoolmaster in Politics
Give 'em Hell Harry
Squire of Hyde Park
Man of Great Heart
That Man in the White House
Silent Cal
Red
Tricky Dick
Ike
Little Magician
Great Emancipator
Old Buck
Honest Abe

Sage of Montpelier
Father of Constitution
Old Man Eloquent
Long Tom
Sage of Monticello
Duke of Braintree
Father of American Navy
Surveyor President
Sword of the Revolution
Canal Boy
Preacher President
Dark Horse President
Fraud President
Old Three Stars
American Caesar
Wool Carder President
Bachelor President

Specific References

When assignments are used for practicing a specific skill, they are often taken by the classroom teacher from a manual or a textbook. The problem is that every student is asked to answer the same (or one of two or three) questions. Sometimes under these circumstances only a few of the students do the work and much copying or sharing of answers is done. If the classroom teacher wants each student to benefit fully from the activity, then each student must have an individual question to answer although these answers will come from the same reference book. This is not as difficult a task for the classroom teacher as it would at first seem.

Use a form that can be duplicated which organizes the information to be checked; i.e., answer to the question, the source used, the volume and paging consulted. Then consult the reference the students are to use taking down a list of terms or entries and their paging. This becomes the answer sheet and also the assignment sheet from which the blank forms will be filled in for the students. A new list should be used with each classroom group and each year. Or at least the fill-ins should be different enough that the students consider them to be completely changed.

In some instances, the assigning of a letter to use when the student selects a topic to verify will be enough to establish independent work (page 109). This small amount of additional effort on the part of the classroom or library media teacher results in much more learning by the students.

Dictionaries, Language
References, and Quotations
Worksheet

Name_____

Date _____

1. Using the *Dictionary of Americanisms,* find the earliest date re-
cording the use in print of the expression_____
   Ans._____ Page(s)_____
   In what writing is it found?_____
   _____

2. Give the derivation of the word_____
   Ans. _____
   Ref. used_____ Page(s)_____

3. Using a dictionary of eponyms, provide the name of the person
alluded to by the word _____ Ans._____
   Ref. used_____ Page(s)_____

4. Using a dictionary of acronyms, provide meaning of the
acronym _____
   Ans. _____
   Ref. used_____ Page(s)_____

5. What is the origin (not derivation) of the phrase_____
   Ans. _____
   Ref. used_____ Page(s)_____

6. Using a thesaurus, provide an alternative word for each of the
parts of speech applicable for the concept word_____
   Noun_____ Verb_____
   Adjective _____ Adverb_____
   Other_____
   Ref. used_____ Page(s)_____

7. Using a dictionary of catch phrases, provide the origin and
meaning of the phrase_____
   Ans. _____
   Ref. used_____ Page(s)_____

8. Using a specialized dictionary, provide the meaning of
   _____ Ans. _____
   Ref. used_____ Page(s)_____

9. What is the symbolism of _____?
   Ans. _____
   Ref. used_____ Page(s)_____

10. Using a reference about the development of the American
language (such as *I Hear America Talking*), locate a lengthy arti-

cle (several pages) on the topic _____

Ref. used_____ Pages_____

11. Using quotation books that are arranged by subject, choose a subject and locate one prose quotation and one poetic quotation dealing with your chosen topic. Provide name of the author and source.

Subject_____

Prose Ans._____

Ref. used_____ Page(s)_____

Author_____

Poetic Ans._____

Ref. used_____ Page(s)_____

Author_____

12. Using the concordance of quotation books, locate the source of the following fragment. Underline the key words that appear in the concordance._____

Ans. _____

Ref. used_____ Page(s)_____

Yearbooks, Statistics,   Name_____
Handbooks, Worksheet   Date _____

1. Using *Facts on File,* choose a topic that can be followed for a
   period of five years (five-year indexes available). Provide a
   precis of the coverage of your topic. Note kind of coverage and
   changes (if any) in emphasis or terminology. Explain the index
   coding for a single entry. List the years used as well as pages and
   subject headings used.

   _____
   _____
   _____
   _____
   _____
   _____
   _____
   _____
   _____
   _____
   _____
   _____
   _____
   _____
   _____
   _____
   _____

2. Using the *Stateman's Yearbook* (19___), give the following
   information for*_____. Page(s)_____
                          (country)
   Population _____ Area_____
   Currency unit_____
   Two natural resources _____ and _____
   Name of their ambassador to the United States_____
   Embassy address_____
   Official name of the country_____
3. Using the *Historical Statistics of the United States,* find the price of
   *_____ per _____ in _____
      (commodity)   (measure)   (date)
   Ans. _____

   _____
   *Teacher should fill in blank with a different specific for each student.

Page(s)_____

4. How many immigrants from*_____ in _____?
   (country)   (date)

   Ans._____

   Page(s)_____

5. Using the *United States Manual* (formerly *United States Govern-ment Manual*), choose a committee or agency about which you know little and answer the following:

   Committee/Agency: _____

   When established?_____

   Mandate? _____

   Regional offices?_____ If yes, where is the one closest to you?_____

   Who heads it?_____

   Who/where is the Washington, D.C., contact?_____

   Page(s)_____

Fine Arts and Recreation
References Worksheet

Name_____

Date _____

1. Find a detailed article on the art topic_____
   _____
   Ref. used_____ Page(s)_____
2. Find a lengthy article on the composer_____
   Where is there a complete listing of his works?_____
   Ref. used_____ Page(s)_____
3. Find an extensive article of the development of the_____
   Ref. used_____ Page(s)_____
4. In the field of theater, identify_____
   Ans._____
   Ref. used_____ Page(s)_____
5. Locate historical information on_____
   Ref. used_____ Page(s)_____

History, Social Studies, and　　Name_____
Curiosities References　　　　Date _____
Worksheet

1. Choose a topic in history that appeals to you. Assemble a bibliography on the topic that includes a reference of each type listed below.
   Topic_____
   Bibliography:
   　　Multivolume history_____ Page(s)_____
   　　Specialized single volume_____ Page(s)_____
   　　Historical dictionary_____ Page(s)_____
   　　Picture history_____ Page(s)_____
   　　Primary source_____ Page(s)_____
2. Using a specialized encyclopedia of social studies, locate a lengthy article on_____
   Ref.　used_____ Page(s)_____
3. Using Congressional Quarterly *Congress and the Nation*, choose a congressman and note his activity between 1945 and 1976 as covered in this reference. Give a brief precis. Indicate volumes and pages used.

   _____
   _____
   _____
   _____
   _____
   _____
   _____

4. Using the United States Supreme Court case identified below, provide the following information.
   Case_____
   Case content_____
   Date of decision_____ Importance of decision_____
   _____
   Name of chief justice of court_____
   Ref.　used_____ Page(s)_____
5. Using *Famous First Facts*, choose a person_____
   How many "firsts" are attributed to this person?_____
   Choose a town_____

How many "firsts" are attributed to this town?_____
Name one "first" that occured on your birthday (not necessarily
year). _____
Now, locate this "first" in the topic index and provide as much
of the who, what, when, where, why, and how as is given for it.

_____
_____
_____
_____
_____
_____
_____
_____
_____

Philosophical, Mythological,   Name_____
and Biblical References   Date _____
Worksheet

1. Using an encyclopedia of philosophy, locate a significant article
   on the philosophy of_____ *
   Ref. used _____ Page(s) _____
2. Using a Biblical concordance, locate the quotation provided.
   Give full information, i.e., complete name of book chapter, and
   verse numbers in the Bible.
   Quotation: _____ *
   Ans._____
   Ref. used _____ Page(s) _____
3. Using a Biblical dictionary, provide identification for the term
   provided.
   Term:_____ *
   Ans._____
   Ref. used _____ Page(s) _____
4. Identify the mythological character given below. Be sure to in-
   clude the mythology from which the character comes as well as
   his role.
   Character:_____ *
   Ans._____
   Ref. used _____ Page(s) _____

---

*Teacher should fill in blank with specific problems for each student.

Assigned letter_____
A. *Short Story Index* and Supplements Volume used_____
   Page(s)_____
   1. Choose an author whose name begins with your assigned letter.
      Author _____
      List two short story titles by this author that can be found in two different collections and give the name of the collection and complete bibliographic information for it.
      a. Story _____
         Collection _____
         Bibliographic information_____
      b. Story _____
         Collection _____
         Bibliographic information_____
   2. Choose a subject beginning with your assigned letter.
      Subject _____
      Give title and author of two stories dealing with that subject.
      a. Title_____ by_____
      b. Title_____ by_____
B. Play Indexes
   1. Choose an author whose name begins with your letter.
      Author _____
      Give name of one play by this author that appears in a collection.
      Title _____
      Give title and bibliographic information for the collection in which this play appears.
      Collection _____
      Bibliographic information_____
      Play index used_____ Page(s)_____
   2. Using a second *Play Index* volume, choose a subject that begins with your letter.
      Subject_____
      Give author, title, collection, and bibliographic information for a play on this topic.

Author _____

Title _____

Collection _____

Bibliographic information_____

Play index used_____ Page(s)_____

C. Poetry Indexes

Using Granger's *Index to Poetry*, select a subject beginning with your letter.

Subject _____

Choose one poem from the list under that subject and for it give the following:

Poet's name_____

Title of poem_____

Name a collection of poetry in which this poem is printed:_____

_____

Select a first line of a poem.

_____

For it give the following:

Poet's name _____

Title of poem_____

Full bibliographic information for one collection in which the poem appears. List the code used.

Code:_____

_____

_____

Materials in Collections
Worksheet II

Essay and General Literature Index indicates the locations of chapters within books that are on specific topics. These sources would be most difficult to locate without using this type of index.

Make choices using your ASSIGNED LETTER_____

1. Use the *Essay and General Literature Index*. Choose a topic (not a person)_____
   and find two references given for it.
   a. For portion: Inside author_____
      Inside title_____
      Author _____
      Title _____
      Publishing info._____
      E&GLI volume_____ Page(s)_____
   b. For portion: Inside author_____
      Inside title_____
      Author _____
      Title _____
      Publishing info._____
      E&GLI volume _____ Page(s)_____
   Use an author of your choice._____
   Select an individual work by the author._____
   Locate a source of criticism dealing with this work._____
   _____
   _____
   _____

   E&GLI volume _____ Page(s)_____

An annual index is provided for *New York Times*. This index is annotated; that is, the content of the article is described in the index. Often abbreviations are used in these annotations and they are understood through context. In more recent years the length of the article is indicated by using the letters S, M, or L within parentheses.

2. Use a *New York Times Index*. Choose a topic of interest._____
   Year_____ Page(s) _____
   Explain the information given in the annotation._____
   _____

Length of article_____ Give location of article in the *New York Times* and explain each element of the location code.

_____

_____

For bibliographic purposes, where will you find the title and author of the article?_____

_____

What indexes to the *New York Times Index* are available to you?

_____

English Search Projects and Worksheets

A number of the activities will be similar in structure. They vary according to requirements, showing ways of adapting the same approach or process technique to the ability level of the students.

Definition of a Concept Search Project

Topic

You are to address the concept of heroism. Although you may approach the subject from almost any point of view, it is expected that your paper will arrive at some kind of definition of the term. In other words, the reader needs to know what the concept of heroism means to you, whether you believe in it or not.

Suggested Approaches

These are only a few suggestions. If you have other ideas, use them.
  a. Talk about one of your heroes or heroines and why he or she fits your definition of heroism.
  b. Argue that the word *hero* does not apply in the 1980's. Explain why it does not.
  c. Discuss the differences between other cultures, times, etc., in their ideas about heroes. Compare another culture with the United States, *i.e.*, Khomeini versus Carter.

Paper Requirements

Your paper must include three quotations from a minimum of *three* of the books which will be shown to you in class. You must use at least one prose quotation and one poetic quotation. The third quotation may be either prose or poetry. You must footnote each quote, and your paper must include a brief bibliography at the end. Follow the style sheet.

Senior Citizens' Contributions Search Project

Topic

Each one of you will be assigned a famous senior citizen to investigate. Using library media materials you will ferret out facts of their lives. While you are reading about your persons' lives, I would like you to focus on the latter part of their lives (last twenty years) to see if you can discover whether or not they were more productive, just as productive, or less productive as they got older. Support your opinion with specifics. After you have gathered this data, you will construct your paper. The paper will conclude with your answering the questions, "How has this person's life affected my life?"

Paper Requirements

Before you enter the library media center, however, you must construct an attack outline which will guide your search in a scholarly manner. The outline should be based on a series of questions you hope to answer such as the "5 W's"—who, what, when, where, why or how. You will not know the answers to these questions at the time you construct your attack plan.

Search Requirements

Your research should include one reference from each of the following types of materials:
   a. Biographical reference
   b. Specialized reference dealing with person's field
   c. *New York Times* article—obituary, if dead
   d. Periodical article

NOTE TO TEACHER: Students were assigned a person by drawing one photograph from a face-down stack of portraits selected by the teacher from the portrait file. Persons were selected about whom there would be enough material available and especially because of their impact upon current society.

American Author Search Project

Purpose

The purpose of this project is twofold: to introduce and/or strengthen various library skills and to enrich your knowledge of six well-known American authors—Ambrose Bierce, Sherwood Anderson, F. Scott Fitzgerald, Ernest Hemingway, Richard Wright, and John Updike. You will be exploring the following areas: biography, literary criticism, social history, and literary history.

Approach

You will work in teams, with each team taking a single author. Thus, in the fourth period class there will be six groups of four people, and in the sixth period class there will be five groups of four and one group of three. I will keep a record of each person's aspect of the research. (Different responsibilities will be given for future assignments using a similar structure. At the end of the year, each student will have engaged in each type of search.)

Schedule

By the end of the *first week*, you will have jotted down some of your sources on note cards (tentative bibliography); *i.e.*, books, magazines, newspaper articles, etc., that relate to your author.

By the end of the *second week*, you will have written an outline of the information you expect to "dig out" during this study. There will be lots of class time in the library in order for us to do this.

In the *third week*, you will take notes on your author on note cards.

Then, during the *fourth week*, we will have oral group presentations so that everyone will benefit from all the work that has been done. At this time you will submit a bibliography stating the particular sources you used for your information.

Grading

Every aspect of this project will be graded—outline, tentative bibliography, note cards, oral presentation, and bibliography. Each segment will be turned in on the due date announced.

SAMPLE CLASS ASSIGNMENT SHEET*

	Hemingway	Bierce	Anderson
Biography			
Criticism			
Social history			
Literary history			

	Fitzgerald	Wright	Updike
Biography			
Criticism			
Social history			
Literary history			

*By entering one student's name in each block of the grid, twenty-four different assignments can be made.

"Macbeth" Search Project I

Assignment

Write a search paper no less than seven typewritten or ten hand-written pages in length. Title page, footnotes, and bibliography pages are in addition to the above.

Use the card system explained in class to prepare outline, tentative bibliography, content notes, draft, completed paper, and final bibliography.

Use *The Research Paper From Start To Finish* (Margaret M. Starkey. New York: American Book Co., 1978.) as the style sheet for bibliographic form.

Search Requirements

1. Use fifteen reference sources (minimum) representative of the following types of reference materials:
   a. Biography
   b. Literary handbook
   c. Literary history
   d. Literary criticism
   e. Theater history
   f. English history
   g. Quotation books
   h. Periodical
   i. Newspaper
   j. Primary source (NOT the play text)

   Use five additional sources determined by the thrust of your paper. This is a total of twenty sources.

   NOTE: Should there be any questions about the use of sources and the acknowledgment of this use, the student will be expected to show where the information used came from before the grading will be done. Therefore, be sure to keep careful and accurate bibliographic references should you need to return to them for future discussion with the teacher.

2. Prepare note content cards with at least one from each reference source type represented in your tentative bibliography.

   Code content cards to outline (which will have been approved before selecting tentative bibliography sources and which will be turned in with note cards).

3. Write draft; revise and write final paper; prepare notes; prepare final bibliography, which is attached to final paper.

Due Dates

_____ Class lecture to lay base for project
_____ (or earlier) Acquire approval of outline and thesis statement (This must be done before starting to assemble tentative bibliography.)
_____ Tentative bibliography completed and approved
_____ First draft of paper (This can be done earlier.)
_____ Final paper

Suggested Topics

1. Character development of Lady Macbeth
2. Macbeth/McBird
3. Why does a good man become evil? Use Macbeth as an example.
4. Trace the deterioration of Macbeth. Cite influences.
5. The good man suffers from the evil of others (McDuff, for instance).
6. "Heavy is the head that wears the crown." Explain.
7. The true history Shakespeare used as his source (Holinshead's Chronicles)
8. How accurate is Macbeth historically?
9. Cawdor Castle: the current Thane of Cawdor lives there today.
10. Warfare of the period
11. Theatrical role of the witches
12. Superstition of the period
13. Shakespearian theater: its structure.
14. Great Macbeth actors
15. Change in interpretation of the role: Macbeth
16. Change in interpretation of the role: Lady Macbeth
17. "Macbeth shall never vanquished be until Great Birnam Wood to high Dunsinaine Hill shall come against him." Explain.
18. Music of Shakespeare's plays.
19. Economic structure of the feudal system: king to peasant
20. The Moors: Shakespeare, Bronte, and Doyle
21. Costuming for Shakespearian productions: 1600 to present
22. Elements of religion in Macbeth
23. Critics' views of Macbeth

Grading

Outline and thesis statement 5%
Tentative bibliography 15%

Form
Completeness of references (15 required types plus 5)
Note cards and first draft 15%
    Cards coded to outline
Final paper...45%
Footnotes...10%
    Form
    Completeness (direct and indirect quotations/plagiarism)
Final bibliography 10%
    Form
    Alphabetic arrangement
    All required reference types represented

"Macbeth" Search Project II

Assignment

Select a project from the list below and prepare it. You will need to find information about the subject of your project. This means that you will need to use the library media center and some class time will be given for this, although it may not be enough to complete the project.

Content note cards and a bibliography will be turned in when your project is presented. Due dates will be announced.

Projects

1. Draw architect's plans for a Shakespearian theater. Attach an explanation of the theater design and a brief biography of Shakespeare.
2. Make a model of a Shakespearean stage. Explain the use of the levels.
3. Construct a set of any scene from *Macbeth*. Attach a written explanation of the significance of the scene.
4. Make a portfolio or poster illustrating Elizabethan dress. Attach a written explanation and description of items illustrated.
5. Make five posters advertising five different Shakespearean plays. Posters must include information about content of plays.
6. Prepare an oral presentation of at least ten minutes on the subject "Was Shakespeare really Shakespeare?"
7. Design and construct an Elizabethan costume in miniature to fit a figurine. Attach an explanation of how the clothes illustrate the social position of the wearer.
8. Prepare an oral presentation of at least ten minutes on any aspect of Elizabethan life that interests you.
9. Make a Shakespearean dart board illustrated with sketches of the different characters from *Macbeth*. Label the game, "Is this a dagger I see before me?"
10. Plan an Elizabethan dinner. Construct a menu, list the courses you would serve, and explain in writing how the dishes were prepared. Prepare one dish for sampling by the class.
11. Make a collection of Elizabethan pastimes and amusements, explaining the rules for each. Use posters or diagrams to illustrate the games.
12. Learn ten quotable quotations from Shakespeare.
13. Make an illuminated manuscript of a famous Shakespearean

quotation using Elizabethan style lettering. Attach a brief
biography of Shakespeare.

14. Write a ballad telling of the life and death of Macbeth.
15. Draw at least three cartoons using Shakespearean quotations as
    punch lines.
16. Write at least five ads advertising modern products using a
    Shakespearean quote or scene as the gimmick.
17. Write a paper (three to four pages) discussing some aspect of the
    history of the English language.
18. Write a short biography (three to four pages) of the life of
    Elizabeth I.
19. Write a short biography (three to four pages) of the life of
    Shakespeare.
20. Group Project: Choose a scene from *Macbeth* and prepare a
    dramatic reading to be presented to the class. Group must meet
    with teacher for conference before proceeding and before
    presentation.

British Poets Search Paper

Topic: Major British Poets

Choose a poet from provided list and research poet according to suggested process. Choose an approach and/or thesis that interests you.

Assignments

It is crucial that you do each assignment and hand it in on time. This project is based upon a step-by-step process. The text to be used is *The Research Paper from Start to Finish*. Please keep all mimeos and old outlines, everything you do regarding this project, in folders provided for that purpose.

1. Due_____
   Read chapters 2, 3, and 4 in text. Hand in tentative thesis (see page 42) and attack outline.
2. Due_____
   Read chapters 5 and 6. Pay special attention to "Don't Plagiarize." Hand in tentative bibliography cards. Be sure to use correct bibliography form. You must submit at least 15 sources. Ten of these sources must come from the following types of references:

Biography	Social History
Geography	Literary Handbook (Benet's
Quotations	*Reader's Encyclopedia*)
Literary History	Newspapers
Literary Criticism	Periodicals
	Primary Sources

   The other five may come from your choice of sources
3. Due _____
   Content cards and source cards, completed and coded.
4. Due _____
   Revised outline and bibliography (typed)
5. Due _____
   Final paper 6 to 8 typewritten pages in length (double spaced)

Major British Poets

No two people may choose the same poet.

Elizabethans	*The Romantics*
William Shakespeare	William Wordsworth

Elizabethans cont'd

Thomas Wyatt
Henry Howard, Earl of Surrey
Sir Philip Sidney
Edmund Spenser
Thomas Campion
Christopher Marlowe

Seventeenth Century

John Donne
Andrew Marvell
George Herbert
Abraham Cowley
Ben Jonson
Richard Lovelace
Robert Herrick
John Milton
John Dryden

Eighteenth Century

Alexander Pope
Thomas Gray
Robert Burns

Revolutionary

William Blake

Romantics cont'd

Samuel Taylor Coleridge
George Gordon, Lord Byron
Percy Bysshe Shelley
John Keats

Victorian

Alfred, Lord Tennyson
Robert Browning
Matthew Arnold
Emily Bronte
Christina Rossetti
Oscar Wilde
Thomas Hardy
Gerard Manley Hopkins
A.E. Housman
Lewis Carroll

Twentieth Century

William Butler Yeats
T.S. Eliot
Rupert Brooke
W.H. Auden
Stephen Spender
Dylan Thomas
Alastair Reid

British Author Search Project

Topic: British poet, novelist, or essayist from 1800 to present

Assignments

Due dates will be given for each of the following.

1. Choose a broad subject; *i.e.*, a British author (no duplicates).
2. Read primary source (original work of the author).
3. Put together a tentative (working) bibliography on three-by-five index cards using the proper form.
4. Read any four of the literary criticism sources or other sources in your tentative bibliography and summarize them in no more than ten lines. (This preliminary reading is to enable you to choose a narrow subject and focus for your paper.)
5. On the basis of what you have found in your preliminary reading of secondary sources, choose a narrow subject and a specific focus or approach. For example: (a) You have already chosen a novel or other subject you wish to write about. That is your broad subject. (b) Based upon your reading, now choose a particular incident, character, or technique (the ending, the setting, etc.). This is your narrow subject. (c) The next step is to decide on what basis, what particular aspect of the narrow subject is interesting. Is it of psychological, moral, historical, or geographical interest? (There are countless other possibilities.) Or do you want to examine what makes it interesting, attractive, distasteful, funny, mistaken, or whatever else you find it. This particular single aspect of your narrow subject is your focus.
6. Write a tentative introductory paragraph for your paper. It should define the exact limits of your paper, give some kind of thesis statement (*i.e.*, what your paper will prove), and indicate how you propose to develop your argument (*i.e.*, how the paper will be structured). The introductory paragraph may be modified in light of later research.
7. Complete research, paying attention only to those sources that contain material relevant to your narrow subject and focus.
8. As you do the research, keep content cards (three-by-five) of opinions, quotations, proofs, etc., that may be useful to you. These content cards will be inspected before you write the paper.
9. Modify your tentative introductory paragraph if necessary. Add to it an indication of how you propose to develop your argument (*i.e.*, give a brief account of how the paper will be structured).

10. Submit final bibliography acceptable to specifications. A total of ten sources is required. Several of the following sources should be represented.
   a. Books
       (1) Literary handbook
       (2) Literary history
       (3) Literary criticism (four required. See #4 above).
       (4) Social history
       (5) Geographical reference
       (6) Biographical reference
       (7) Quotation
   b. Periodicals (academic, magazines, Victorian fiction, etc.)
   c. Newspapers (*New York Times Index*, etc.)
   d. Nonprint (teacher's notes, records, private conversations) These should be quoted as sources.
   e. Contemporary Reference*
       (1) Written by or about the author
       (2) Personal anecdote
       (3) Judgment of the author by friends
       (4) Newspaper account
       (5) Someone on the scene
11. Write the paper, making full use of content cards and referring constantly to the primary source.
12. List footnotes on separate sheet of paper.
13. List bibliography (which must match prescribed number and variety of entries) in alphabetical order on a separate sheet of paper after the footnotes.
14. Compose table of contents page to be inserted after the title page.
15. The outline page or pages will follow the table of contents page.
16. Number the table of contents and outline page(s) with Roman numerals, small letters, (i, ii, iii) typed in the center at the bottom.
17. Type complete paper in the order indicated above (*i.e.*, title page, table of contents, outline, text of paper, footnotes). Add bibliography (which has already been submitted and checked) at end.
18. Do not number footnote and bibliography pages.

---

*This teacher prefers to use the term "primary source" for the author's writing being studied (*see no. 11*), and to use "contemporary reference" for firsthand accounts often referred to as primary sources.

Literary Criticism Worksheet   Name_____

Date _____

For the author listed, create a bibliography that includes all the major references in the library.

Author _____

Dates_____ Country_____ Type of writing_____

Biographical References

Author		Title		Page(s)

Literary History References

Call #	Author	Title	Volume(s)	Page(s)

Literary Criticism References

Call #	Author	Title	Volume(s)	Page(s)

"800's" Worksheet

Name_____

Date _____

Using the term _____, compare its coverage in two
literary handbooks and in a literary history.

Literary Handbook

Author_____ Call #_____

Title _____ Page(s)_____

Coverage: _____
_____
_____
_____
_____

Literary Handbook

Author_____ Call #_____

Title _____ Page(s)_____

Coverage: _____
_____
_____
_____
_____

Literary History

Author_____ Call #_____

Title_____ Volume(s)_____ Page(s)_____

Coverage: _____
_____
_____
_____
_____

Quotations Search Project

Quotation books are usually arranged by theme or subject. Bartlett's *Familiar Quotations* is arranged by author, and other quotation books include an author index, usually placed between the excerpts and the concordance. The students can be made aware of the arrangement of quotation books, that there are collections that emphasize poetry or prose or that are limited to a single theme, and that the source of the quotation excerpt is provided at the end of each excerpt. The use of the abbreviation *Ibid.* should be thoroughly understood.

After instruction has been provided, students may be asked to select one quotation that appeals to them and to explain in writing why they find meaning in it. Or they may be asked to select two quotations on the same theme and write about the similarity or difference in the thoughts expressed.

So that many students do not choose the same topic, they may be asked to choose a topic that begins with the same letter as their own last name. Another approach is to assign a letter of the alphabet to each student, and if the class is large enough to require the repetition of a letter, the classroom teacher can exercise care regarding which students have the same assigned letter.

Some reference titles which should be useful in this project are listed below. Obviously, if the class is working from theme, Bartlett's is going to be less useful.

Poetry References

Bartlett, John.   *Familiar Quotations*
Evans, Bergan.   *Dictionary of Quotations*
Stevenson, Burton. *Home Book of Classical Quotations*
                   Home Book of American Quotations

Prose References

Adler, Mortimer. *Great Treasury of Western Thought*
International Dictionary of Thoughts
Kenin, Richard.   *The Dictionary of Biographical Quotations*
What They Said in 19— (a series begun in 1963 and published annually).

Proverbs References

The Macmillan Book of Proverbs, Maxims, and Familiar Phrases

Quotations Worksheet　　　　Name_____
　　　　　　　　　　　　　　　Date _____

Assigned letter_____

Choose a subject beginning with your assigned letter.

Subject _____

Using a quotation book arranged by subject, select two quotations, write them below, and give bibliographic information for the original as well as for the quote in the quotation book.

Quotation book used_____ Page_____
1. First quotation:_____

　　_____

　　Author of quote_____ Work taken from_____
　　Exact location in work (if given)_____
2. Second quotation:_____

　　_____

　　Author of quote _____ Work taken from_____
　　Exact location in work (if given)_____

Find a proverb or maxim based on the same subject.

Proverb/Maxim: _____

_____

Quotation book used_____ Page_____

Using a prose quotation book, choose an author or speaker whose last name begins with your assigned letter. Locate a quote by him and give a precis of the quote. Identify the surrounding circumstances when and where quote was first made, if this information is given.

Author of quote_____
Quotation: _____

_____

Precis:_____

_____

Word Origins Search Project

There are many books of word or phrase origins (as differentiated from word derivation). Students are usually fascinated by these anecdotes. Most students will have had some previous exercises using an unabridged dictionary to find derivations and trace a word's travel from language to language. Some will have heard the story of the Earl of Sandwich's hunting trips and the alleged creation of the word *sandwich*—as well as the sandwich itself.

Assignment Suggestions

1. Students may be assigned a word or phrase taken from the books of word origins available (either assigned through drawing by lot or chosen within the "assigned letter" framework) and asked to read about its origin and report to the class.

2. Students may be asked to become creative, develop a new word or phrase of their own, and write up an explanation of its origin.

Suggested References

Funk, Wilfred. *Word Origins And Their Romantic Stories*
Funk, Charles Earle. *Thereby Hangs a Tale*
                Horsefeathers
                Hog on Ice
Limburg, Peter. *What's in the Names of Birds?*
Morris, William and Mary. *Dictionary of Word and Phrase Origins*
    (three volumes)
Potter, Stephen and Sargent, Laurens. *Pedigree: The Origins of Words From Nature*
Asimov, Isaac. *Words of Science*
          Words from Myths
          Words in Genesis
          Words from Exodus
          Words on the Map
          Words from History

Picture History Search Project

English teachers have frequently used a print or painting as a subject for a written assignment. The student may be asked to describe it, react to it, or explain it. The same thing can be done with a photograph.

Another approach is to provide the students with picture histories and allow them to select a picture that appeals to them as a subject for a written assignment. The advantage here is that the student learns about the existence of picture histories, becomes somewhat familiar with them, and also learns how to footnote the picture or illustration that was chosen to write about.

This becomes a skill the student can use in other classes. Picture histories are most useful in social studies or any other situation in which social history is examined.

Poetry Definition Worksheet   Name_____

Date _____

Use literary handbooks or poetry handbooks to help find definitions
for each of the following terms as it relates to the study of poetry.

I. Rhythm
   A. Accent
   B. Foot
   C. Scanning
      1. Iambic
      2. Trochaic foot
      3. Anapestic foot
      4. Dactylic foot
   D. Meter
      1. Monometer
      2. Dimeter
      3. Trimeter
      4. Tetrameter
      5. Pentameter
      6. Hexameter
      7. Heptameter
      8. Octameter

II. Rhyme
   A. Rhyme scheme
      1. End rhyme
      2. Internal rhyme
   B. Blank verse
   C. Free verse

III. Stanza form
   A. Couplet
   B. Quatrain

IV. Sensory Impression
   A. Onomatopoeia
   B. Alliteration

V. Figures of speech
   A. Simile
   B. Metaphor
   C. Personification

VI. Kinds of Poetry
   A. Narrative poetry
      1. Epic
      2. Ballad
      3. Folk ballad
      4. Literary ballad
   B. Lyric poetry
      1. Ode
      2. Elegy
   C. Didactic poetry

Letter Writing Search Project

Letter writing appears in almost every English curriculum. When this project is being done is a good time to tie in the reading of letters written by famous—and some not-so-famous—people.

Many anthologies include a selection from Lord Chesterfield's *Letters to His Son*. There are collections of famous letters that contain Lincoln's letter to Mrs. Bixby, and many biographies reprint letters that are of interest. From the point of view of search, the student can be made aware of the collections available, the value of letters as a primary source, and our historical dependence on the information provided by letter writers.

Suggested References

Allilueva, Svetlana. *Twenty Letters to a Friend*

Baker, Carlos, ed. *The Private Hemingway: From His Unpublished Letters, 1918–1961*

Browne, Eliza Southgate. *A Girl's Life 80 Years Ago*

Elbogen, Paul. *Dearest Mother: Letters from Famous Sons to Their Mothers*

Holmes, Oliver Wendell, Jr. *Touched with Fire: Civil War Diary and Letters*

Jones, Katherine. *Heroines of Dixie: Confederate Women Tell Their Story of the War*

Litchfield, Henrietta. *Emma Darwin: A Century of Family Letters*

Maser, Werner. *Hitler's Letters and Notes*

Mitchell, Margaret. *Gone with the Wind Letters, 1936–49*

Plath, Sylvia. *Letters Home: Correspondence, 1950–1963*

Schuster, Max. *Treasury of the World's Great Letters*

Social Studies Search Projects and Worksheets

Activities included here range from work on highly specific topics to those that are interdisciplinary in their approach. Many call for creative interpretations that allow the student to apply humor. Humor cannot exist without awareness of the situation being lampooned, so learning must take place. Why shouldn't learning be fun?

Book Critique Search Project

This assignment can apply in any discipline. The student is provided a set of requirements, *i.e.*, the types and number of materials to be used and the specific approaches to use or topics to address. The format used for this history assignment will be useful applied to material available in other disciplines. There is always a point of view of the author, and either agreement or disagreement with that point of view can be expressed by others.

To assist the students with the assignment, an approach guide sheet was prepared and the process was discussed in the classroom by the library media teacher.

Assignment

The project for the first marking period is a critical book review. Your choice of book may be a biography, an historical novel, or any nonfiction that you find interesting. Any person, event, or subject related to ancient history as we are studying it in this course is acceptable. Your text contains several bibliographies and a table of contents which might be helpful in making a selection of topic. All books must be approved by the teacher.

Your critical book review should range from 750 to 1000 words in length and include the following:

1. Title page
2. Statement of the issue that the author is analyzing in his book
3. Statement of the author's point of view
4. Analysis of the author's arguments in support of his/her thesis
5. Summary of what other authors have said about the issue (a minimum of three other sources must be used)
6. Summary of the historical background against which the book is written (material will be gathered from other sources)
7. The student's point of view on the issue with explanation of why this view is taken
8. The student's critique of the author's style, organization, ability to sustain interest, etc.
9. Bibliography

Sample Search Approach Guide Sheet

TOPIC: Atlantis

BOOK READ: Chapin, Henry. *The Search for Atlantis*. New York: Crowell-Collier Press, 1968. 105 pp.

METHOD AND MATERIALS USED TO SEARCH CRITIQUE

1. Card catalogue: Looked under *Atlantis* in the subject file. Found five books:
   a. a complete book: Ferro. *The Autobiography of a Search* (913.3)
   b. four partial books: (1) Donnelly. *Atlantis, the Antidiluvian World*, the preface and the six chapters of part one (913.3) (2) Time-Life, The Emergence of Man Series, *Lost World of the Aegean*, chapter four (933.9) (3) *New York Times. Science of the Times*, "Atlantis Recaptured" (500) (4) Vitaliano. *Legends of the Earth*, chapter nine, "Lost Atlantis Found?" (398)
2. Periodicals: Used *Reader's Guide* and found two magazine articles:
   a. "Atlantis: Bimini hoax." *Sea Frontiers*. May 1978, pp. 130–34.
   b. "Solving the Lost Continent Mystery." *Reader's Digest*. August 1978, pp. 128–33.
   Separate Index to *Horizon*: Reference to Spring, 1972 issue, 4 pages.
3. Newspapers: Used *N.Y. Times Index*, 1979. Found three articles: May 21, 14:1 (M); Aug. 29, 4:3 (M); Aug. 29, 4:3 (S)

PROBLEMS RELATED TO TOPIC AND BOOK

1. Historical Conflict: There appear to be three ideas about where Atlantis may have been. One is the island Thera in the Aegean Sea; another is the Azores in the Atlantic Ocean; and the third is the island of Bimini in the Caribbean.
   a. Support for Thera theory: The island collapsed in an earthquake and volcanic eruption. Archaeological work has been done there.
   b. Support for the Azores theory: Plato's history of Atlantis and Donnelly's account.
   c. Support for Bimini theory: Ferro and Grumley's ideas and search (1968) and Edgar Cayce's prophesy that Atlantis would reemerge in 1968 or 1969.

2. Identities: Know something of each of the people, where they lived, and when.
3. Scientific Facts and Conclusions about the Mystery
   1. Thera earthquake and volcanic explosion
   2. Atlantic Ocean seafloor
   3. Alterations in land masses in Caribbean

Historical Fiction Search Project

Social studies teachers often assign the reading of historical fiction by their students. A followup activity that uses the materials of the library media center is to ask the students to verify the facts presented in their novels.

The novels will be set within a given time frame and country, and then will be filled with references to real people. Searching for verification of the facts used in the piece of historical fiction becomes an exercise based on the structure of reference books. Collected biography tends to be arranged similarly by country and date. The same is true for multivolume histories. When social histories are also included, the search becomes a practical exercise in the use of reference materials.

To write a paper defending one's findings calls for the citing of references and certainly precludes the use of a review or book jacket blurb merely to summarize the story line.

When the historical fiction is being selected, it is helpful to use thematic fiction guides for suggestions and the identification of specific coverage. Awareness and use of such guides becomes an additional skill for the student. A helpful selection tool is *Fiction Catalog* published by H.W. Wilson Co. which includes an extensive subject index. Historical fiction is found by looking under the country name and then the chronological subdivisions, or under related historical terms such as *chivalry* or *crusades*.

World War II Search Project*

You are to select a topic from the list below on World War II from the start of American involvement and prepare an oral report on it. The oral presentation will be limited to a maximum of five minutes. Your talk should be clear enough to give the significance of the topic you are covering, but do not go into details that will be lost on those who are listening. Structure your presentation tightly and logically. This calls for use of an outline.

You will have to do some research to get down the basics. Plan to use the maps in the classroom for demonstrations.

	Date	Name	Topic
1.	_____	_____	North Africa
2.	_____	_____	Sicily
3.	_____	_____	Italy
4.	_____	_____	Italy
5.	_____	_____	Italy
6.	_____	_____	Landings in southern France
7.	_____	_____	Normandy
8.	_____	_____	The drive inland
9.	_____	_____	Drive to the Siegfried Line
10.	_____	_____	Arnheim
11.	_____	_____	Battle of the Bulge
12.	_____	_____	Bombing—day light raids (SAC)
13.	_____	_____	OSS
14.	_____	_____	Naval war in the Atlantic
15.	_____	_____	Pearl Harbor
16.	_____	_____	Fall of the Philippines (Bataan, etc.)
17.	_____	_____	Midway
18.	_____	_____	Coral Sea, Bismarck Sea, New Guinea
19.	_____	_____	Coral Sea, Bismarck Sea, New Guinea

_____

*Dates are filled in by teacher to match the classroom coverage schedule before students sign for the topic.

20. _____ _____ Guadalcanal and the Solomons
21. _____ _____ Guadalcanal and the Solomons
22. _____ _____ Marianas (Guam, etc.)
23. _____ _____ Gilberts and Marshall Islands (Tarawa)
24. _____ _____ Reconquest of the Philippines
25. _____ _____ Iwo Jima
26. _____ _____ Okinawa
27. _____ _____ Burma and China Theaters
28. _____ _____ A-bomb, surrender of Japan

Politics Search Project

Assignment

Write a search paper no less than six typewritten or eight hand-written pages in length. Title page, footnotes, and bibliography pages are in addition to the above.

Use the card system explained in class to prepare outline, tentative bibliography, content notes, draft, completed paper with notes and final bibliography. Use *The Research Paper From Start To Finish* as the style sheet for bibliographic forms.

Search Requirements

1. Use six reference sources (minimum) representative of the following types of references:
   a. Biography
   b. Specialized dictionaries
   c. Periodicals
   d. Newspapers (*New York Times* and *SIRS*)
   e. Primary source
   f. Specialized references (different for various topics)
      (1) *Congressional Quarterly* publications
      (2) Connecticut State Statutes
      (3) *Editorial Research Reports*
      (4) Nonprint items
      (5) Specialized encyclopedias and books (not general encyclopedias)
2. Prepare note content cards with at least one card from each of the required reference source types. Content must be coded to the outline (which will have been approved before selecting sources and which will be turned in with the note cards).
3. Write draft; revise and write final paper; prepare final bibliography and note section.

Due Dates

Outline and thesis statement approved _____

Tentative bibliography (six types of sources) _____

Rough draft and note cards _____

Completed paper, footnotes, and bibliography _____

Grading

Outline and thesis statement   5%

Tentative bibliography   15%
   Form
   Representative sources
Draft and note cards   15%
   Notes coded to outline
Writing of paper   45%
Footnotes   10%
   Form
   Completeness (direct and indirect quotations)
Final bibliography   10%
   Form
   Alphabetized
   All required references represented

United States History Search Project

Assignment

You are to prepare a report on the period between 1870– 1917 when America comes of age. Listed below are suggested topics from which to choose. There are others which are not listed, but which would be interesting and perfectly acceptable as long as cleared with the teacher first. Topics are assigned on a first come, first served basis. Only one student may select each topic.

You are to use a minimum of five sources; only one of these may be a general encyclopedia. The report is to be four to six pages typed or written in ink. It is to include a bibliography page and footnotes where necessary.

You will have one library day a week for the next four weeks to gather information on your topic. On the third library day, each student is to have prepared an outline which will be checked for your progress. This will be a quiz grade.

The assignment (outline) will be marked down five points for each day and ten points for each weekend that it is late thereafter.

Topics

1. Prepare an eyewitness account of Dewey entering Manilla Bay. The American and Spanish fleets at Santiago.
2. Investigate such things as violence, mob actions, wars, and police actions in the years 1870–1917. Was America more or less civilized one hundred years ago than it is today?
3. Compile a "Who's Who Among Black Americans" for the years 1870–1917. Refer to any copy of *Who's Who in America* as to style of entry and the type of information that should be included.
4. Write an account of the rise and fall of Jim Crow laws between 1870 and 1960. See Woodward's *Strange Career of Jim Crow*.
5. "We want to make a machine that will last forever," announced Henry Ford. "It doesn't please us to have a buyer's car wear out or become obsolete." Read about the history of the automobile and find out what happened to Henry Ford's good intentions. How did the concept of "planned obsolescence" thwart his goal of a car that would last forever? When and why did Ford have to alter his master plan?
6. Were the politics of the Gilded Age as bad as they have often been made out to be?

7. Was Teddy Roosevelt really imperialistic?

8. How did the progressivism of Theodore Roosevelt differ from that of Woodrow Wilson?

9. Investigate the work of the Rockefeller Foundation in its fight against disease.

10. What was student life like in the nineteenth century American university? How did it differ from what you know of university life today? See Bragdon's *Woodrow Wilson: The Academic Years*, Chapters 2, 6, 8, and 9.

11. Why did Bryan lose the election of 1896? What did McKinley represent to his supporters? See Glad's *McKinley, Bryan, and the People*.

12. Read the 1912 platforms of the Democratic, Bull Moose, and Socialist parties in Commager's *Documents of American History*. How do they differ? In what ways are they virtually the same?

13. Look into the dramatic and often volatile history of the "Wobblies" (as the members of the IWW were called). Consider their leaders, their purposes, their activities, their victories and defeats, their songs. Were they representative of an alien "ism," or were they as "American as corn on the cob?" See Dulles' *Labor in America* and Bayback's *History of American Labor*.

14. Theodore Roosevelt is said to have created "a condition of excitement and irritation." Did he do more than this? What really was his contribution to American reform, both as President and as leader of the Bull Moose Party?

15. In what ways did Roosevelt, Taft, and Wilson expand the powers of the President?

16. The platform of the Populist Party called for a number of reforms. Choose any one of these demands and trace the degree to which this demand was or was not met in later years. In the course of the research you will find some of the populist demands were adopted by one or more of the other national parties. It is not enough to show merely that the demands were or were not accepted. You are to seek reasons and explanations. This topic may be chosen by several students so long as each student has chosen a different reform.)

17. How does the town you live in relate to this period of American history? Consider immigration, growth of industry, big business, railroads, etc.

18. Write a history of boxing between 1870 and the present. Include

a comparison of an outstanding player of the sport in the years before 1900 and a modern counterpart.

19. Write a history of tennis as for boxing, above.
20. Investigate the evolution of the sewing machine. Who was the principal inventor. Names that will be important in this report include Walter Hunt, Elias Howe, Isaac Merrit Singer.
21. Contact the League of Women Voters and read state or local histories to find out how long women have been part of the political scene in your state. What issues or causes have they championed?
22. Since the sinking of the British luxury liner *Lusitania*, many suspicions have been voiced concerning its actual cargo, the purpose of its voyage, and alleged prior knowledge of the attack. Read several accounts of the last voyage, including contemporary accounts (*New York Times*, etc.), and try to determine to your own satisfaction the real circumstances behind this significant international incident.
23. William Jennings Bryan as Secretary of State
24. America's China Policy in this period
25. Japanese immigration to the west coast
26. The "Rough Riders"
27. Phineas T. Barnum—his role in our history
28. The fate of the American Indians
29. The Beef Barons—Swift and Armour meatpacking companies
30. The "yellow journalism" of William R. Hearst and J. Pulitzer
31. Any of the true wilderness adventures by James Willard Schultz

Chronologies Worksheet   Name_____

                            Date _____

Using your assigned year_____, select an event that appeals to
you: _____

Compare the coverage of that event in the chronologies listed below.

	Chronology	*Pages with listings*	*Coverage/ Content*
1.	*Langer's Encyclo-pedia of World History*	1. _____	1. _____
2.	*Timetables of History*	2. _____	2. _____
3.	*Storey Series*	3. _____	3. _____
4.	*Steinberg's Histori-cal Tables*	4. _____	4. _____

**Using the chronology "Who Was When," choose someone born in
your assigned year and give his/her name and profession.**

Name_____ Profession_____

List two contemporaries born ten years later and their professions.

1. Name_____ Profession_____
2. Name_____ Profession_____

Middle Ages Group Search Project

Assignment

1. You will be divided into groups and assigned general topics. You will divide the general topic into specific topics, one per person in the group. This should be done as much as possible according to individual interests of group members. These decisions must be made and clearly understood before going to the library media center.

2. Your group will then go to the library to research your topic in depth. Your text provides general information that will give you an adequate background on the period. Your research will supplement and expand this background for greater understanding of the topic. You are to use at least two library sources (absolutely no general encyclopedias) per person in the group. A bibliography of your group's sources is to be submitted the day of your presentation.

3. After gathering information on your topic, you will present it orally as a group report. Each group has half period (twenty minutes) for the presentation. The second half is devoted to discussion of the topic by the class. Each person in the group speaks on a specific topic with a logical order of sequence being followed so that the entire class gains knowledge of the topic. Each person will have only three to five minutes to speak! Try to be interesting in your presentation of your research. Be organized! Be prepared! Be clear!

Samples: Diary of a Knight: "My armour is rusted and my horse is busted." or

Manor politics: "Water under the gate"

Requirements

1. Bibliography—two sources per person
2. Oral presentation
3. Full attention while others present their topics

Grading

No credit will be given to those who read their reports. You will be graded on the following:

Content—what you say—result of your search	50%
Organization—how well prepared you are	25%
Understanding—how well you know your topic	25%

Topics
A. Feudalism—political
    1. Feudal hierarchy—outline of how the system worked
    2. King—function, duties, role
    3. Lords and nobles—functions, duties, role
    4. Knights—functions, duties, role
    5. Serfs—functions, duties, role
B. The manor and the Medieval town—economic
    1. Manorial system—physical outline of the manor setup
    2.   —how the system functioned
    3. The castle—physical outline and setup
    4.   —how life functioned within—importance of castle
    5. Medieval town—physical setup
    6.   —life within the town—function and importance of the town
    7. Medieval guilds
C. Medieval culture—social
    1. Dress—Lords, knights, serfs
    2. Food
    3. Chivalry—courtly love (manners, relations between sexes)
    4. Sports—jousting, bearbaiting, falconry, tournaments, etc.
    5. Entertainment—ballads, minstrels, feasts, fairs
    6. Women's role
D. Medieval art and learning—social
    1. Education of boys and girls—what was taught
    2. Universities—what was taught, where, life of student
    3. Romanesque architecture—description of style with examples
    4. Gothic architecture—description of style with examples
    5. Literature—manuscripts, ballads, poems, etc.
    6. Medieval philosophy—known as "Scholasticism"—describe and give examples

Renaissance Period Search Projects

Assignment

Below is a list of topics covering the Renaissance period. Choose one of these topics as an individual project. Each project differs in its format, but they all have three things in common. They require research, thinking, and your creativity!

Requirements

1. Outline of the topic which becomes the rough draft of the project.
2. Bibliography of at least three sources used in developing the project.
3. Completed project. See the specific requirements for your topic. Emphasize thought and creativity.

Topics

1. Interview one of the following Renaissance men or women. Ask questions that will reveal their life and work and why they are famous.
   a. One of the Borgias
   b. Machiavelli
   c. Lorenzo de Medici
   d. Pope Julius II
   e. Pope Leo X
2. Draw diagrams or make models of types of ships, sailing instruments and kinds of maps used by the fifteenth and sixteenth century explorers. Give a written explanation to match each.
3. You are a travel agent putting together a package deal, a tour of Renaissance Florence. Show your prospective clients that this is definitely a place to see. Include in your written tour guide a description of the government, culture, layout, spots of interest, things to do, important personalities to look for.
4. "The Young and the Restless" is the title of your new soap opera about Renaissance women. In the episodes, explore the new liberated women's clothes, education, role in society, and relations with the opposite sex. Develop a character and use her to portray this information.
5. You are fashion editor for *Vogue* magazine. Your assignment is to do a feature article on the latest fashions in Florence, Italy (fourteenth or fifteenth century) or England (sixteenth century).

Choose one class and show both men and women's fashions. You should use diagrams, pictures, and/or models (one or all) to illustrate your article. In the story include how these clothes reflect the status of the people in their society.

6. The Museum of Modern Art has asked you to write an article analyzing a great work of Renaissance art. Choose one of the following artists and one of their masterpieces. As an art critic, explain what characteristics make the work typically Renaissance; include a brief biography of the artist and a history of the masterpiece.

   a. Michaelangelo   n. Bosch
   b. Da Vinci   o. Durer
   c. Botticelli   p. Masaccio
   d. Cellini   q. Uccello
   e. Ghiberti   r. Fra Filippo Lippi
   f. Brunelleschi   s. Della Francesca
   g. Raphael   t. Bellini
   h. Giotto   u. Van Eyck
   i. Verrocchio   v. Bruegel
   j. Ghirlandajo   w. El Greco
   k. Titian   x. Holbein
   l. Tintoretto   y. Vasari
   m. Rubens

7. You are a young, upcoming reporter for the *Florence Post*. Your editor has sent you to cover a story which is breaking fast —the Italian Watergate—the scandal of how the de Medicis rose to power in Florence. Investigate the story, talk to the people involved, and cover the important events and the results of the scandal (the de Medicis' rule in Florence). Format: a news article, complete with headlines, dates, etc.)

8. You are in charge of the "Roasting of Savonarola, the Mad Monk of Florence." Investigate his work, give a brief history of his rise to and fall from power. Invite pertinent guests to the roast to help toast Savonarola.

9. You are the roving reporter for *Playboy Magazine*. You are investigating what type of man reads *Playboy* in the Renaissance. He is, of course, the playboy of all times, the courtier. Interview Castiglione who wrote *The Book of the Courtier* and find out what the Renaissance playboy wears, his education, manners, sports, relations with women, etc.

10. You are doing a feature article for *House Beautiful Magazine* on

the Renaissance home. Choose one fine home in either England (sixteenth century) or Italy (fourteenth or fifteenth century). Explain the layout of the home, its location, the kinds of furnishing, etc. Of course, illustrate your article!

11. You are food editor for *Good Housekeeping Magazine* and must do an article on the food of the Renaissance. Choose either England (sixteenth century) or Italy (fourteenth or fifteenth century) and describe typical dishes of the day. Include a sample menu, ingredients, how the dishes were prepared; and, for extra credit, prepare one of the dishes for sampling by the class.

12. You are an attorney from the Patent Office investigating Gutenberg's new invention, the printing press. You must prove this is a worthwhile invention and deserving of a patent. In your report to the Patent Office, tell what the invention looks like, how it works, its benefits, drawbacks, and longrun effects on society. Also, include a brief biography of the inventor.

13. Do the same as #12 for one of Da Vinci's inventions.

14. You are an aspiring writer studying Renaissance literature as a reflection of man's new outlook on life. Read excerpts from one of the following authors and tell how each reflected this changed outlook on life. Write a critique of the piece explaining what made it typically Renaissance in style and content. Also, include a brief biography of the author.

    a. Boccaccio   f. Rabelais
    b. Cellini   g. Shakespeare
    c. Petrarch   h. Milton
    d. Machiavelli   i. Erasmus
    e. Cervantes

15. Galileo is being tried by the church for heresy. You are on the council investigating his crimes and will determine whether he is excommunicated. In your report to the Pope, explain Galileo's work and discoveries and give a brief biography of him. Submit at the end of your report your conclusion of his guilt or innocence based on your findings. You may use diagrams to document your evidence.

16. You are on the committee to award the Nobel Prize for _____ during the Renaissance. Choose one of the scientists below as your nominee for the prize. Investigate his work and discoveries, and give a brief biography of him. Use diagrams to support your

candidate. Present the information as a nomination proving that your candidate is the best choice.

a. Galileo   f. Kepler
b. Harvey   g. Versailius
c. Boyle   h. Descartes
d. Bacon   i. Leeuwenhoek
e. Copernicus   j. Newton

17. You are chair of the Committee to Save Venice (which is slowly sinking into the sea). Report to the President on why Venice should be saved. Present evidence showing Venice's glorious history (through the Renaissance), the artistic treasures of the city, and the layout of the city.

18. You are a music critic for the *Rolling Stone*. Follow one of the two hot new composers listed below. Interview this Renaissance musician and find out what his sound is all about.

a. Vivaldi
b. Palestrina

19. You are a spy for the CIA (Concerned Italian Associates) sent on a mission to investigate a group of hired Italian hit men known as the *condottieri*. Report to your bureau chief on their purpose, activities, location of operations, leaders, weapons, clothes, etc. File this Top Secret.

20. You are first mate on the Santa Maria. Write a diary or journal describing Columbus's first voyage to the New World. Include description of ships, conditions on board, sailing techniques, provisions needed, and a brief history of the undertaking (how it was financed, successes, failures, etc.).

21. Do the same as #20 for another explorer of the time.

22. You are a journalist for *MS* magazine covering a very controversial story, "Did women have a Renaissance?" The widely held belief is that women of all classes improved their status and expanded their roles in society during the Renaissance. You must uncover the "truth." You have been given your title; fill in the rest.

23. You are the roving reporter for *Glamour* magazine. You are investigating what the upper, middle, and lower class woman's life was like during the Renaissance. Interview a woman from each class and explain her status in society, her role in society (political, economic, and social), her education, relationships with men, etc.

24. You are Barbara Walters or Morley Safer sent to interview one of the women listed below for a story, "Famous Women of the Renaissance," for the network. In your interview ask questions that will uncover the following information: Why is the woman famous or infamous? What are her achievements or contributions to society? Biographical information (date and place of birth, family status, etc.).

    a. Lucrezia Borgia   d. Vittoria Celanna

    b. Beatrice D'Este   e. Queen Jeanna of Naples

    c. Isabella D'Este   f. Catherine de Medici

25. Any other idea you have had approved by your teacher.

England and France through Napoleon Search Project

1. Make a model or drawing of a warship of Sir Francis Drake's fleet as it would have been constructed when he defeated the Spanish Armada in 1588. This is to be accompanied by an oral explanation in front of the class.
2. Write a newspaper account of the defeat of the Spanish Armada and give an explanation of the importance of the event.
3. Write a history of the Tower of London and its role throughout English history. (Optional: Include a sketch of the Tower.)
4. Write a ballad or short story telling the story of the six wives of Henry VIII. Sing or read this to the class.
5. Prepare a document showing the English Bill of Rights. Explain how it came into being.
6. Make a chart or poster of English Parliament explaining how it came into existence and its function today.
7. Design and construct an Elizabethan constume in miniature to fit a model. Explain how the clothes illustrate the social position of the wearer.
8. Prepare an historically sound written debate either supporting or rejecting the idea that Elizabeth was England's first monarch.
9. Make a creative presentation of the conflict and conspiracy between Mary Queen of Scots and Elizabeth I over the throne. (Suggestions: a story, song, poem, or drawing with explanation) (Discuss your plan with teacher for approval.)
10. Prepare a biographical sketch of the activities of one of the following during the period given:
    Edward IV, 1461-83
    Edward V, 1483-(his death is very significant.)
    Richard III, 1483-85
    Henry VII, 1485-1509
    Henry VIII, 1509-47
    Edward VI, 1547-53
    Mary I, 1553-58
    Elizabeth I, 1558-1603
    James I, 1603-25
    Charles I, 1625-49
    Oliver Cromwell, 1649-60
    Charles II, 1660-85
    James II, 1685-88

Mary II, 1689–93
William II, 1689–1702 (William and Mary rule together.)
Sir Francis Drake
Sir Walter Raleigh
Anne Boleyn
Lady Jane Grey
Sir Thomas More
John Knox

11. You are first mate to either Sir Francis Drake or Sir Walter Raleigh. Write a ship's log of their journeys and discoveries. Include a biography.

12. You are a reporter for the *London Times*. Write a news account of any one of the following:

> Charles I's beheading
> Cromwell's takeover
> The Puritan Revolution
> William and Mary's arrival in England

13. Interview Sir Thomas More the day before his death.

14. Take a photograph or draw a sketch of a Baroque or Rococo style building and describe the significant architectural features in this example.

15. Create four cartoons showing aspects of Louis XIV's reign. (Suggestions: how he ran his government, amused himself, regulated business, controlled religion) Explain each cartoon and its significance.

16. Prepare a menu of a classical French meal (like one served to Louis XIV) and give a brief history of French cooking. Prepare one dish and serve it to class. (Discuss this with teacher.)

17. Prepare a biography of Joan of Arc and show a creative version of her death.

18. Make a detailed sketch of Versailles, accompanied by a brief history of the palace. A slide show or picture show can take the place of the sketch.

19. Make a poster telling the story of St. Bartholomew's Day Massacre. Give a brief description of the event and its importance.

20. Make a detailed study of the Louvre. Provide diagrams and drawings. Provide its history, how it was built and by whom.

21. Make a detailed study of Fountainbleau, home of French kings and chief glory of French Renaissance architecture. Provide sketches or assemble a picture or slide presentation.

22. Make a study of one Baroque or Rococo artist and one of their paintings. (Check choice of artist with the teacher.)
23. Write a biographical sketch of one of the following:
    Francis I
    Catherine de Medici
    Cardinal Richelieu
    Colbert, Minister to Louis XIV
    Louis XIII
    Louis XIV
    Louis XVI
24. Write a soap opera about Louis XIV's many mistresses.
25. Prepare an interview with Louis XIV on his feelings about being king.
26. You are a reporter for *Paris Match*. Prepare an interview with Napoleon. Discuss his life and accomplishments.
27. You are TV anchor for the local Waterloo station. On the 6:00 p.m. news, you must report the Battle of Waterloo. Include brief background history.

Mathematics Search Projects

Students are sometimes given names of mathematicians to find in biographical references, and books of recreational mathematics are used to provide challenge of the puzzle type. Much more than this, however, can be done to involve math teachers and math students with the library media center staff and materials. The two activities reproduced here are from *Mathematics Teacher* magazine, often a source of additional ideas for projects—as are the journals of the other professional disciplines.

The "Great Mathematical Scavenger Hunt" by Sharyn Evans of Middletown, New Jersey, was used exactly as it was presented in the magazine by the teachers in our school. Unfortunately, the first thing that the library media teachers knew about the project was when students, already at work on the fill-ins for the formula, started asking for information. Two of the questions (e and m) could not be answered in our school collection. We were able to enlist the help of someone who spoke Oriental languages and of a larger library for these answers. If the library media teachers had known about these problems in advance, we might have arranged for substitutions that would have provided the same numerical quantity from the references at hand.

"Support Your Local Library: A Task-Card Project for Mathematics Students" by Betty Krist, Mary Ellen O'Neill, and Lawrence Feldman of West Seneca, New York, also attracted the attention of our mathematics department. It is presented here with an explanation of what they did with it to show how an idea can be adapted to suit local needs.

Using the idea in the article as a base, the classroom teacher and the library media teacher worked out a variation. Basically, the classroom teacher decided to have each student devise ten questions, each of which would require a mathematical answer and all of which would cause her students to learn about the use of materials in the library media center. In order to assure that students would be required to use the collection broadly, it was decided to ask the student to make each question representative of the materials organized under a different Dewey classification. Also, all questions had to be devised using materials that were in the high school library media center.

Students were provided with an outline sheet describing the contents of the Dewey categories (as follows) and the library media teacher visited the classroom with a booktruck filled with examples of basic reference books. The arrangements and limitations of these standard references were described, and the possible types of questions that could be devised were discussed. These were to serve as examples only; students were encouraged to be as creative as possible.

It was the classroom teacher's plan to mark students for the first quarter on the quality of the questions they devised. The next quarter, questions would be exchanged among students so that everyone would have the opportunity to find the answer to someone else's set of questions. The student's success in finding correct answers would be given a mark for the second quarter. These activities provided two rounds of examination of basic references in each of the Dewey classification divisions.

The Great Mathematical Scavenger Hunt*

TABLE 1

$$z = \cfrac{\sqrt{\cfrac{\dfrac{fs}{\left(\dfrac{o}{(t+m)}\right)} + k \cdot \dfrac{ij(a-b)(y-u')^o}{nc}}}{h - r\dfrac{(v+x-p)}{i}}}{\dfrac{h - r\dfrac{(v+x-p)}{i}}{e-(d+v+rf)} \cdot \dfrac{q^w - g}{l^w - g}}$$

a = a speed of 60 mph that corresponds to how many km/h?

b = normal body temperature in centigrade.

· c = the length of a side of a cube whose volume is 125 cm³.

d = the number of nanograms in one microgram.

e = the value of:

𝍣
Ｆ
ᕤ
大
子
四

f = the value of this Mayan symbol: ⠢

g = the value of 239_{twelve} in base ten.

h = the value of 5736_{eight} in base ten.

i = Ikumi, the Lamba word for what number?

j = $.\overline{076923}$, the same as what fraction?

k = birth year of Mikolaj Kopernik.

l = the sum of the fifth row of Pascal's triangle.

m = the number of pounds sterling that the Irish Sweepstakes Derby ticket cost in 1972.

n = the zip code of Annette, Alaska, minus the zip code of Kotlik, Alaska.

o = the number of blue stripes in the Cuban flag.

p = the year Phineas Barnum was born.

q = the number of subsets in a set with five elements.

r = 13(mod 7) = ?

s = the value of $_3P_2$.

t = the density of water in g/cm³ (at 3.98°C).

u = the number of letters in the name of the artist who created the lithograph *Reptiles*.

v = the number of the computer Hal in *2001—a Space Odyssey*, divided by 10.

w = the number of letters in the animal name for 1980 according to the Chinese lunar calendar.

x = population of Hallettsville, Texas, in 1950.

y = the number of times greater the diameter of Jupiter is than the diameter of Earth is when rounded to the nearest whole number.

Adaptation of Task-Card Project

1. You will devise a set of ten questions each of which requires a mathematically related answer.
2. Each question will be drawn from a different Dewey category. (See information provided below.)
3. All questions must be able to be answered through use of the materials in the library media center.
4. Take notes regarding the purposes, limitations, and arrangement of the basic reference materials discussed by the library media teacher.
5. Be as creative as possible in devising your questions, but remember that the questions must be good with no necessary elements left out. Remember, also, that you will be answering someone else's questions next term.

Dewey Classification Categories

000 *General references* (N.B.: Do not use general encyclopedias for this project), *journalism, flying saucers.* Because this section is small, combine with fiction (by theme, possibly).

100 *Philosophy.* Philosophy is a big word for ideas. Mathematical ideas are found in philosophy encyclopedias under the names of the mathematician and/or the concept.

200 *Religion.* Bible, mythology. Consider the Book of Numbers in the Bible.

300 *Social Sciences.* Aspects of living; i.e. law, education, race problems, statistics, government, taxes, money, inflation.

400 *Language.* Numbers in other languages (even extinct ones); the origin of word phrases (tangent, hypotenuse, etc.)

500 *Pure Science.* History of science, mathematics, astronomy, physics, chemistry, earth science, botany, zoology.

600 *Applied Science.* The mathematics and physics becomes engineering; biology becomes medicine; etc. Inventions.

700 *Fine Arts and Recreation.* Perspective, rules of proportion in art; musical mathematics; sports records, playing fields, etc.

800 *Literature.* Poetry about mathematics or mathematicians; letters of mathematicians; writers who were mathematicians such as Lewis Carroll or Omar Khayyam.

900 *History, Biography.* 925's collected biography of mathematicians and other scientists.

Sample Questions and Answers*

Mathematics Task Card 1

Answer the following questions on a separate sheet of paper. You must also give the title, author (or volume), and page number for the location of each answer.

1. What is the fundamental theorem of arithmetic?
2. A famous unsolved problem is called Goldbach's conjecture. What is it?
3. What is topology?
4. What was the inscription over the entrance to Plato's Academy?
5. Write 9/7 as a continued fraction.
6. What is 10^{100} called?
7. What is the answer to Martin Gardner's puzzle about Bronx versus Brooklyn?
8. Why was Pierre Simon de Laplace not killed during the French Revolution?
9. How many different ways are there to make change from a dollar bill?
10. In the Snow White system of numeration, "10" could equal what decimal numbers?

Correct answers for Task Card 1: *

1. Every integer n greater than 1 can be factored into a product of primes in only one way. *What Is Mathematics?* Courant and Robbins, p. 23.
2. Every even number except 2 is the sum of two primes. *Invitation to Mathematics*, Glenn and Johnson, p. 53.
3. Topology deals with properties that remain unaffected when geometric shapes are bent, twisted, stretched, shrunk, or otherwise deformed. *The Realm of Science*, Vol. 3, p. 90.
4. Let no one enter who is ignorant of geometry. *The Language of Mathematics*, Land, p. 175.
5. *Continued Fractions*, Olds, p. 3:

*Krist, Betty; O'Neil, Mary Ellen; and Feldman, Lawrence, "Support Your Local Library: A Task-Card Project for Mathematics Students," *Mathematics Teacher* 73 (October 1980): 516–17.

$$1 + \cfrac{1}{3 + \cfrac{1}{1 + \cfrac{1}{1 + \cdots}}}$$

6. One googol. *The Lore of Large Numbers*, Davis, p. 25.
7. The Bronx train comes 1 minute after the Brooklyn train. *Mathematical Puzzles and Diversions*, Gardner, p. 33.
8. He was needed to calculate trajectories for the artillery. *Mathematics*, Bergamini, p. 128.
9. 292. *Mathematics of Choice or How to Count without Counting*, Niven, p. 107.
10. 4 or 8. *Mathematical Puzzles and Pastimes*, Bakst, p. 68.

Science Search Projects and Worksheets

Although the activities included here were designed for chemistry classes, the exercise sheets can easily be adapted for physics, biology, or earth science. The classroom teacher compiled a bibliography of materials in the library media center that were considered most useful for the assignments. This list follows for teacher reference or for distribution to students.

An exercise was designed requiring the use of the specialized dictionary or handbook for the discipline. Note the layout of the worksheet which makes checking of the answers easier for the teacher. Another exercise centers on biography and leads the students to specialized collected scientific biography. A third deals with finding current information on societal problems related to the discipline. The other two are interdisciplinary in nature.

BIBLIOGRAPHY FOR CHEMISTRY LIBRARY ASSIGNMENTS

The following bibliography should be useful to you in beginning your chemistry library assignments. There are many more resources available in the library which are not listed here. Do not hesitate to ask the librarians for assistance in finding the materials you need.

CRC Handbook of Chemistry and Physics. Lists physical and chemical constants of elements and compounds. Good for definitions of chemical terms.

Essay and General Literature Index. Indexes books and parts of books in all fields.

General Science Index. Indexes scientific periodicals.

Reader's Guide to Periodical Literature. Indexes periodicals in all fields.

Scientific American: Cumulative Index 1948–1978. Indexes articles from the *Scientific American* magazine.

422 Asimov, Isaac, *Words of Science and the History Behind Them.* Fascinating book giving the roots and histories of scientific terms.

500 *Illustrated World of Science Encyclopedia.* Text very clearly written. Very well illustrated. Each section contains a section of a scientific dictionary which is complete in the full set. Volumes ten, eleven, and twelve deal with chemistry specifically. Volumes nineteen and twenty contain scientific biographies.

500 *Life Science Library.* A twenty-five-volume set with a cumulative index entitled *A Guide to Science.*

500 *Science of the Times.* A survey of articles which have appeared in the *New York Times* on a variety of scientific subjects. Good for current environmental issues.

503 *New Junior Encyclopedia of Science.* A profusely illustrated set with a simple text covering general science.

503 *Van Nostrand's Scientific Encyclopedia.*

507 *McGraw Hill Dictionary of Scientific and Technical Terms.*

508 Shapley, Harlow (ed.), *The New Treasury of Science.* A series of scientific articles dealing with many aspects of science. Contains a good section on the manmade elements.

509 Schwartz, George, *Moments of Discovery: The Development of Modern Science.* Describes the work of many well known scientists.

509 Williams, L. Pearce, *Album of Science—The Nineteenth Century.* A well illustrated history of nineteenth century scientific developments.

539.7 Gallant, Ray, *Explorers of the Atom.* A succinct history of the development of atomic theory.

540.9 Asimov, Isaac, *A Short History of Chemistry.*

540.9 Ihde, Aaron, *The Development of Modern Chemistry.* An excellent history of chemistry. Appendix I lists elements and their discoverers.

543 Longgood, William, *The Poisons in Your Food.* A report on chemicals used in the food industry.

546 Asimov, Isaac, *Building Blocks of the Universe.* A descriptive coverage of the elements, their history, uses, etc.

546 *The Elements: Builders of the Universe.* A descriptive coverage of the elements with many illustrations.

546 Ley, Willy, *The Discovery of the Elements.* A good description of the history and discovery of each element. Includes many interesting anecdotes.

546 Sampson and Low, *The Elements and Their Order.* A description of the preparation, properties, and uses of each element. Written very simply.

546.1 Friend, J. Newton, *Man and the Chemical Elements.* A history of the discovery of the elements.

641 *Sourcebook on Food and Nutrition.* Includes much useful data on food, food additives, and the dangers and nutritional value of each.

925 *Asimov's Biographical Encyclopedia of Science and Technology.*

925 *Dictionary of Scientific Biography.*

Chemistry Handbook Worksheet

The *CRC Handbook of Chemistry and Physics* is a valuable tool for students and professionals in scientific fields. Each year a new edition is published with small changes from the previous year. The exercise below is to acquaint you with the type of information available in the handbook.

Use the "CRC Handbook" to answer the following questions. Put the page numbers in the parentheses provided.

1. The edition and years of the handbook are_____.
2. The index covers pages _____ to _____.
3. The element radium was discovered in the year
   _____ (　　).
4. The melting point of sodium chloride is_____ (　　).
5. The density of carbon tetrachloride is_____ (　　).
6. The solubility of sodium hydroxide is_____ (　　).
7. The formula for the oxo acid, rhenic acid, is
   _____ (　　).
8. Two common names for sodium sulfate decahydrate are _____ and_____ (　　).
9. The chemical name for the mineral pyrite (fool's gold) is _____ (　　).
10. The atomic mass, half life, and mode of decay of the isotope $^{233}_{92}U$ are_____, _____ and _____ (　　).
11. The common name, molar mass, and boiling point of the organic compound chloroethene are_____, _____, and _____ (　　).
12. According to the formula index of organic compounds, the substance with a formula of C^3H^3N is _____ (　　).
13. The third most common element in sea water is _____ (　　).
14. The composition and the manufacturer of the plastic Plexiglas are _____ and _____ (　　).
15. The chemical resistance of the plastic Polyethylene to strong acids is rated as _____ (　　).
16. The heat of formation of crystalline iron III chloride is _____ (　　).

17. The pH of soft drinks is _____ (   ).

18. Phenolphthalein indicator has an approximate pH range of _____ and a color change of
    _____ (   ).

19. The larger the dissociation constant of an acid, the stronger the acid. Which acid is stronger, iodic acid or nitrous acid?_____ (   ).

20. The specific heat of aluminum at 25°C is_____ (   )

21. The freezing point depression of a 50% by mass aqueous solution of ethylene glycol is_____°C (   ).

22. Ethylene glycol is the active ingredient in what consumer product?_____ (   ).

23. The heat of combustion of methane at 25°C is
    _____ (   ).

24. The dipole moment for water is_____ (   ).

25. The specific gravity of the sulfuric acid in a fully charged battery is 1.275 to 1.380. The percent of sulfuric acid in a fully charged battery solution is
    _____ (   ).

26. The definition of the term dipole moment is_____
    _____ (   ).

27. How many definitions are provided for the term acid?_____ (   ).

28. The percent of sodium by mass in the earth's crust is _____ (   ).

29. Find the vapor pressure of water at 23°C._____ (   ).

30. List the various isotopes of chlorine, giving the mass number of each._____ (   ).

Biographical Search Project

The development of chemical knowledge has a long history of growth, beginning with the ancient Greek philosophers and continuing in research laboratores today.

Investigate the life and scientific discovery of the scientist assigned to you. If possible, include societal and scientific influences which led to the discovery. Report your findings in a short paper, listing at least three references used.

Democritus	Linus Pauling
John Dalton	John Berzelius
J.J. Thomson	Henry Moseley
Ernest Rutherford	Alfred Nobel
Wilhelm Roentgen	Joseph Priestley
Henri Becquerel	Robert Millikan
Marie Curie	Amadeo Avogadro
Pierre Curie	Johann Balmer
William Crookes	Evangelista Torricelli
James Chadwick	Robert Boyle
Werner Heisenberg	Jacques Charles
Phillip Lenard	Stanislao Cannizaro
Neils Bohr	Albert Einstein
Michael Faraday	Joseph Gay-Lussac
Werner Heisenberg	Dmitri Mendeleyev
John Newlands	Max Planck

Chemistry Search Project

The proliferation of chemical knowledge has led to a great many discoveries and products which affect our lives. New knowledge about nutrition and improvement in chemotherapy have increased life expectancy and triggered a population explosion. The development of pesticides may have a serious effect on the environment. The development of nuclear power is highly controversial.

Select a problem from the list below or one of your own choosing and investigate both its positive and negative effects on human life. Report your findings in a short paper, listing at least five references used.

Nuclear warfare
Nuclear power plants
Disposal of nuclear wastes
Industrial wastes and hazards
Environmental chemical hazards
Food additives
Ecological hazards
Dwindling energy resources
Dwindling water resources
Dwindling mineral resources
Dwindling soil resources
Biological hazards of the petrochemical industry
Nuclear waste plants
Environmental impact of the Alaskan pipeline
Aquaculture
Biodegradable detergents
Biodegradable packaging
Environmental impact of insecticides
Environmental impact of herbicides
Deep sea mining
Desertification of the earth's surface

Chemical Elements Search Project I

The names of many elements come from foreign words describing their characteristics. Other elements have been named by their discoverers to honor a person or place.

For the element assigned to you, complete the following:

1. Find the discoverer of the element and the year of discovery.
2. Find the origin of the element's name.
3. Explain why, if you can, the element was given this particular name.
4. Where is your element found in nature?
5. List industrial and everyday uses of the element and its alloys.
6. What environmental problems are associated with the mining, refining, industrial preparation, use and/or disposal of the element?

Chemical Elements Search Project II

Although the exact number that actually exists is not known, at present 105 elements are known. In general, elements have not been named in a systematic way. Some elements, like gold, silver, and iron, have been known as long as recorded history. Many of these elements have symbols which are abbreviations of Latin, Greek, or German words.

For the element assigned to you:

1. Find the original name.
2. Determine the name's country of origin.
3. Determine the original meaning of the name.
4. How does the name describe the element?
5. Find other English words which have the same root and give their meanings.

Elements

Antimony	Sb	Potassium	K
Copper	Cu	Silver	Ag
Gold	Au	Sodium	Na
Iron	Fe	Tin	Sn
Lead	Pb	Tungsten	W
Mercury	Hg		

Art Search Projects

The art teacher wanted students to broaden their use of the library media center and also to have some variety in assignments in their art work. To do this, the teacher began a file of individualized assignments which is added to as new ideas emerge.

The student interested in doing something different or extra may browse through the file selecting an activity that has appeal, or the teacher may assign a given activity to the student. In either case, the activity requires that the students come to the library media center and become involved in examination of some type of reference material.

Art Activity File Samples

The activities that follow are taken from the art teacher's activity idea file.

1. Look through a book on American architecture (720.973) and select an era you like or find interesting. Work out a series of elevation views that would fit comfortably into that era. Use layout/bond paper or pen and ink with washes.

2. Look in a reference book on an era or a country such as *Modern Painting* (759's) or *Spanish Painting*. Select some works and create a painting in the style of those works.

3. From *A Dictionary of American Portraits* by Cirker, select a portrait of a famous American and recreate it in a medium of your choice. (Should you want to have a copy of the portrait on hand, make a photocopy of it. Do not take out the book.)

4. Select a book on a sport of your choice (796's). Without copying any of the illustrations, create a work that could be used in the book.

5. Look through a book on photography (770). Select a photograph you like and recreate it in the stippling technique.

6. From a book on Haiku (895.6), select a poem (or write one yourself in the Haiku style after consulting the book). Write the poem in calligraphy and work an illustration into the project.

7. In *The Encyclopedia of World Art*, Volume X, read the article on mosaics and notice the illustrations. Create an original, contemporary art work in this style using color aide paper.

8. Look through some books on block printing (760, 762, 769) and note the different styles that can be produced by this method. Develop an original sketch that can be translated into a two-color block print.

9. Examine *Fiction Catalog* (Ref. 016). Select a story title and illustrate the title in a specific technique.

10. Find a book on the science or psychology of color (752). Create two identical designs using acrylics; paint them in different color schemes to create two different moods or illusions.

11. Examine books on silk screen printing (764). Using three or more stencils, design a cover for a school yearbook.

12. Locate Marco Matteucci's *History of the Motor Car* (629.2). Select a car and situate it in an environment that would be suit-

able for the era. Execute the work in pen and ink and water-color or in tempera.

13. Find a book on a decade like the Twenties or the Thirties (in the picture histories) or a short-lived era like Art Deco (745.2) or Art Nouveau (709.04). Look through the books to get a feel for the style. Design a fabric pattern that would have been typical for that era.

14. Select a current *Art in America* (Ref. 700). Examine current trends. Create a two- or three-dimensional work that fits into a current trend.

15. Look in a book on philately (796.56). Design a postage stamp (which can be reduced to the correct proportions) that would be suitable for the United States Postal Service.

16. Find a book on stained glass (748.5). With pen and ink and watercolor or tempera, create a design that could be trans-formed readily into the stained glass process.

17. Operas are stories set to music. Look through books on the opera (782.1)—Kobbe is a good one—and design a three-color poster that would be suitable for the story line. (Also see Gallo's *Poster in History, The American Poster Renaissance,* or other books on posters (769).)

Index

Abbreviations, 81–85
Adapting to skill level, 18
Alphabetizing, two ways, 35, 36, 39, 77–80
American Fiction, 25
Art, 105, 172–174
Assigned letter, 100, 109–112
Atlases, 74
Attack outline, 17, 19, 31, 48, 50–52, 55–56, 59, 115

Bibliographic skills, 31–34
Bibliography, final, 65; tentative, 52–54, 56, 59; textbook, 13
Biography, 95–99
Booktruck collection, 14
By and about rule, 45–46

Card catalog, 36–46, 70
Card system, use of, 52–59
Catalog card, 37, 38, 39, 70
Chronologies, 26–27, 147
Class visit to media center, 33–34
Coding, 53, 57, 59
Concept search project, 114
Concordances, 102, 108
Contemporary Literary Criticism, 24, 58
Content notes, 54, 57
Cross references, 22

Departmental standard, 17, 47
Diagnostic testing, 31, 69–76
Dictionaries, 71, 90–94, 101, 108
Due dates, 16, 19, 119

English, 113–134

Essay and General Literature Index, 46, 111

Famous First Facts, 106–107
Fiction Catalog, 139
Fiction, historical, 139
Filing rules, abbreviations, 40; by and about, 45–46; compound words, 42; exceptions, 44–45; Mc–Mac, 39–40; numerals, 41–42; subdivisions, 42–45
Five W's formula, 49–51
Footnotes, 60–64, 132
Format clues, 38

Gardening With Wildlife, 61–63
Grading: assuring integrity, 61, 65, 67; easing load of, 16–19
Granger's Index to Poetry, 110

Idea file, 67, 172–174
Index terminology, 37, 86–89
Indexes, 72–73, 86–89, 109–112
Individualizing assignments, 66–67, 87–94, 97–157
Integrated activity, 10–12
Intradepartmental planning, 15

Letter writing, 134
Library lesson, 12
Library media teacher responsibility, 21, 33–34
Library media teacher in classroom, 10–11
Library of Literary Criticism, 24
Limited materials, 13–16
Limiting topic, 21, 47 ff

Literary criticism, use ot, 24–25
Literary handbooks, use of, 22–24
Location clues, 38

Mathematics, 158–163
Multivolume references, 26

New York Times Index, 72–73, 87, 111–112
Nonprint materials, 38, 47, 64
Note cards, 52–59

Oral reports, 18, 116
Outline format, 75–76; organization, 48–52

Peer expectation, 21
Performance-based tests, 32–33
Periodicals, 27, 86–89
Picture histories, 64, 132
Plagiarism, prevention of, 19, 60–65, 67, 118
Play Index, 109
Poetry handbook, 133
Poets, 123–126
Pre-search preparation, 29–33
Primary sources, 67, 126
Project file, 67, 172–174

Quotation books, 101–102, 129–130

Reader's Encyclopedia, 22
Reader's Guide to Periodical Literature, 45–46, 86–89
Reassurance, 11, 21, 29–30, 33–34, 50
Requirements: bibliographic form, 43, 47, 52–54, 56, 59, 65, 118, 142; due dates, 16, 19; style sheet, 47; types of references, 18, 115, 118, 123, 126–128, 142; written, 17, 114
Responsibilities, 9, 12, 21, 29–30 33–34

Science, 164–171
Scoring sheet, 17, 19
Search guide, 137–138
Search paper defined, 7
Short Story Index, 109
Shorter papers, value of, 15, 16–17
Social studies, 106–107, 135–157
Specialized references, purpose and scope, 38–39
Staggered assignments, 15, 16
Standards, departmental, 17, 47; *See also* Requirements.
Statistical, use of, 103–104
Story of Civilization, 26
Style sheet, 47, 52–53, 118, 142

Tables of contents, use of, 25–26
Teacher responsibility, 9–12, 21, 29–30, 33–34
Thesis statement, 17, 19, 21–28, 58, 119
Time requirements, 34
Time saving tips, 55
Timetables of History, 26
Timing, 13, 16, 17, 18, 116
Topic selection, 10–18, 20–28, 100
Topic sources, 21–28
Types of references, 8, 18, 115, 118, 123, 126–128, 142

Unfamiliar topics, 20–21

Word origins, 131

Yearbooks, 103–104